THE EUROPEAN CHALLENGE

1992

Research on the 'Cost of Non-Europe' Steering Committee

Chairman: Paolo Cecchini
Coordinator: Michael Loy
assisted by: Maria Brindlmayer
Andrea Forti

* * *

Sergio Alessandrini
Michel Aujean
Michel Ayral
Michel Catinat
Paul Champsaur
Jean-Michel Charpin
Michel Deleau
Michael Emerson
Wolfgang Gerstenberger
Philippe Goybet
Peter Holmes
Alexis Jacquemin
Jean François Marchipont
Jacques Pelkmans
Carlo Secchi
Manfred Wegner

The research for this study was funded by The Commission of the European Communities

The European Challenge

1992

The Benefits of a Single Market

Paolo Cecchini
with
Michael Catinat and Alexis Jacquemin

Written by John Robinson

WILDWOOD
HOUSE

Published by
Wildwood House Limited
Gower House
Croft Road
Aldershot
Hants GU11 3HR
England

and distributed by
Gower Publishing Company
Old Post Road
Brookfield
Vermont 05036
USA

Reprinted 1988 four times, 1989 twice

ISBN 0 7045 0613 0

The publishers wish to thank Guillaume·Muller, Head of the Co-ordination and Preparation of Publications division of the European Commission, for his help and cooperation during the publication of this book.

Typeset by Columns of Reading
Printed and bound in Great Britain by
Biddles Limited, Guildford and King's Lynn

Contents

Tables

Charts

A common objective
Jacques Delors
President of the Commission of the European Communities

The countries of the European Community needed a common objective which could raise their sights above daily routine problems and thereby concentrate their energies. It was for this reason that my colleagues and I in the Commission proposed to the Heads of State and Government and to the European Parliament that we should create a truely unified economic area in Europe by 1992.

This large market without frontiers, because of its size and because of the possibilities that it offers for scientific, technical and commercial cooperation, gives a unique opportunity to our industry to improve its competitivity. It will also increase growth and employment and contribute to a better balance in the world economy.

It has a social as well as an economic dimension, and must lead to a more unified Community. The twelve Member States have rightly decided that it should be accompanied by policies that will lead to greater unity as well as more prosperity. They have therefore strengthened Community technology policies and enlarged the resources available for helping the long-term unemployed, youth unemployment and rural development; as well as the backward regions of the Community and those facing major restructuring problems.

This large market that we are creating is of direct concern to every citizen of Europe. It is revolutionary, but it will be achieved both because it is absolutely necessary and because it carries with it the goal of a united and strong Europe.

Foreword
Lord Cockfield
Vice President of the Commission of the
European Communities

We are on the move. The programme for the Completion of the Internal Market by 1992 is now well under way. The programme will be completed, and it will be completed on time. That is the objective set by the Single European Act and that is the objective we must achieve.

No one now doubts the importance of the task or the opportunities it opens up.

It was an act of faith – confidence in the present and faith in the future – that we – the Community – embarked on this task. Now, with the publication of this major study under the skilled and dedicated chairmanship of Mr Paolo Cecchini, we are able for the first time to see the precise measure of what we are going to achieve. Now we have the hard evidence, the confirmation of what those who are engaged in building Europe have always known: that the failure to achieve a single market has been costing European industry millions in unnecessary costs and lost opportunities; that the completion of the Internal Market will provide the economic context for the regeneration of European industry in both goods and services; and that it will give a permanent boost to the prosperity of the people of Europe and indeed of the world as a whole.

The importance of this study, and of what it reveals and confirms, cannot be overestimated. Mr Cecchini and his team have laid before us, in terms which will be clear to every citizen of Europe, the full magnitude of what needs to be achieved in cutting out red tape, in breaking down protectionism and removing blocks on cross-border activities.

But it does not just demonstrate the heavy cost of having 12 separate markets divided by frontier controls. More important by far, it also demonstrates the immense opportunities for the future which the completion of the internal market will open up: opportunities for growth, for job creation, for economies of scale, for improved productivity and profitability, for healthier competition, for professional and business mobility, for stable prices and for consumer choice. In short a prospect of significant inflation-free growth and millions of new jobs.

No other approach to the challenge of Europe's economic future could possibly promise so much. No single Member State on its own could ever generate such a total transformation of its economic performance and prospects. It is only by completing the single European market of over 320 million people that we will make those prospects a reality.

The people of Europe have a right to realise the immense potential which is at present held in check by our internal divisions. Those whom they elect to govern them have a duty to unlock those fetters. This report provides evidence of what is at stake, of what we all stand to gain if they succeed and to lose if they fail. They must not fail us. We must claim our right to the prosperity, the jobs and the secure future for generations to come which this book shows are ours to create. The political courage and determination must be forthcoming.

Acknowledgements
Paolo Cecchini

This book is the thin end of a very large wedge – a wedge of collective effort invested in a research project into the 'costs of non-Europe', which I have had the privilege to direct since its inception in early 1986. My first thanks must therefore go to Lord Cockfield, Vice-President of the Commission of the European Communities, who, in asking me to take charge of this unprecedented endeavour, provided me with what has proved to be a most challenging opportunity.

The offer was so challenging that, before taking it up, I thought it best to take a second opinion about its feasibility – in fact, several second opinions. Fortunately, they proved encouraging, and I am indebted to those who provided them : Robert Toulemon, the Commission's former director-general for industry, internal market and research; François Duchêne who, when at Sussex University, directed a most impressive project on industrial policy in Europe; Sergio Vaccà, vice-rector of Bocconi University in Milan; and Manfred Wegner now of Germany's IFO, and a former colleague when he was the Commission's deputy director-general for economic and financial affairs.

Central to the ensuing effort has been the advisory role played in it by the members of the Steering Committee – the project's intellectual guardians and also, in some important respects, its innovators. His colleagues will forgive me if I make mention here of Michel Catinat whose special contribution, since the very beginnings of the project, was his work on devising the macro-economic evaluation system for the welfare gains provided by the European home market.

Needless to say, the overall economic guidance supplied by Michael Emerson was indispensable, as were the efforts of Michel Aujean and Philippe Goybet and the teams working under them. A number of distinguished economists contributed special studies. Amongst them special mention should be made of Michael Davenport who developed the microeconomic model methodology, and Gernot Nerb who was responsible for the industrial business survey. The work of this team and also colleagues in many

Commission departments, is more fully reflected in the overall economic report on *The Economics of 1992* published in parallel with this book (see Appendix 2).

The project's outstanding results would not have been possible without the exceptional efforts of the coordinating team which Fernand Braun, the Commission's director-general for industry and internal market, put at my disposal.

No praise is high enough for Michael Loy who, after taking over from Jacques Soenens as head of the team in early 1987, shouldered an often nightmarish task with a rare blend of equanimity and success.

The same is true for Andrea Forti and Maria Brindlmayer whose contribution included the challenging and exhausting task of supervising and synthesising the research results in preparation for the book. They also undertook the vital but thankless duty of ensuring effective liaison with the outside consultancies engaged by the Commission for the research project into the costs of non-Europe.

Finally, acknowledgements could not be complete without recognition of the supporting role played by Ursula Nieberding and Isabelle Hariga in the project's administration.

San Feliu de Guixols
February 1988

xvi

Summary and conclusions:
High stakes for Europe: the 1992
challenge – the prize within the grasp

The challenge
This book profiles the European Community home market in the
1990s, the costs of its absence today, and the gains on offer for the
EC economy as a whole once the costs are converted into benefits.
Benefits most obviously for consumers and for companies in the
shape of lower prices and lower costs – but benefits, also, which are
stamped in social and political coinage.

Thus, for the first time for nigh on two decades, the 1990s offer
the outlook of a new springboard for economic policy management
and for major reductions in chronic European unemployment after a
short-term adjustment period. It is, we believe, a substantial story
about a challenging prospect, whose implications spill over EC
boundaries into the global economy. But it has Europe at its centre
and its origin.

The challenge, that of creating by 1992 a single EC home market
by removing the barriers between its twelve national components, is
first and foremost a challenge for Europeans. However, if they
respond robustly, the continent's citizens, companies and governments will do more than realise their collective economic potential as
Europeans. They will propel Europe onto the blustery world stage of
the 1990s in a position of competitive strength and on an upward
trajectory of economic growth lasting into the next century. Such
additional growth, following the progressive impact of EC market
integration, could, in the space of a few years, put between four and
seven percentage points on the Community's domestic product. This
vista is not a tantalising chimera. On the contrary, it is a firm
prospect.

The research
The outlook emerges from an unprecedented research programme,
launched in 1986 by EC Commission vice-president Lord Cockfield.
Its purpose was to provide a solid body of scientifically-assembled
evidence as a means of judging the extent of the market
fragmentation confronting European business and Community

policy-makers alike. In the process, the research has thrown up a vivid illustration and rigorous analysis of the costs imposed on Europeans by the mosaic of non-tariff barriers which – 30 years after the Community's birth – continue to mock the term 'common market'. The findings of this research into the 'costs of non-Europe', are outlined in their essential detail in the pages of this book.

The research is unprecedented for various reasons – first for the sheer size of its scope, but also because of the novelty of the subject-matter and the methodological difficulties that were encountered in making the analysis and calculations based on it. A further problem was the unevenness of the empirical data on European market fragmentation. Yet despite these fragilities, the results that emerge tell an unmistakable story.

They estimate the size of the costs and thus a potential for gains exceeding Ecu 200 billions.[1] This basic benefit, which could be magnified by modestly positive economic policies, is the reward for removing the barriers targetted by the 1992 legislative programme set out in the EC's 1985 White Paper *Completing the Internal Market*.[2] Thus when EC political decisions are taken and the business community has fully adjusted to the new competitive environment, gains of this order of magnitude would be acquired once and for all, meaning that the European economy would be lifted onto a higher plane of overall performance.

The barriers – like border controls and customs red-tape, divergent standards and technical regulations, conflicting business laws and protectionist procurement practice – are well enough known by name. But not until now has their impact, and that of their removal, been charted and costed. These results, the product of the extensive field-work and subsequent analysis, are outlined in Part I, together with illustrations of the workings of non-Europe in a broad range of industries and services.

Likewise, the White Paper's legislative programme for removing market barriers, reinforced since mid-1987 by the Single European Act, is also well known. But what has not been estimated until now is the value of the ultimate prize which Community governments could, by enacting it in full, deliver to Europe's citizens, its companies – and to themselves. Detailed estimates of these overall gains, and the mechanisms by which they are to be realized, are made by two separate but complementary approaches – respectively a micro-economic and a macro-economic analysis – and are presented in simplified form in Part II.

The shock and the prospect
For all the complexities, the essential mechanism is simple. The

starting point of the whole process of economic gain is the removal of non-tariff barriers.

The release of these constraints will trigger a supply-side shock to the Community economy as a whole. The name of the shock is European market integration. Costs will come down. Prices will follow as business, under the pressure of new rivals on previously protected markets, is forced to develop fresh responses to a novel and permanently changing situation. Ever-present competition will ensure the completion of a self-sustaining virtuous circle. The downward pressure on prices will in turn stimulate demand, giving companies the opportunity to increase output, to exploit resources better and to scale them up for European, and global, competition.

However, the effect of the shock is to be gauged not just in terms of the market, and of the companies and consumers who buy and sell there. Its waves will ripple out into the economy at large. By its very size, the shock will have reverberations on general economic management. Over time, creation of a European home market will unbind the macro-economic constraints which have chronically fettered the prospects of sustained growth in Europe for the best part of twenty years.

Public deficits will be eased, under the dual impact of open public procurement and the economy's regeneration. Inflation, traditionally growth's ugly sister, will be cooled down by the drop in prices provoked by open markets. The jolt so imparted to Europe's competitivity should ensure that growth is achieved without damage to the Community's external trade position.

But, perhaps most important of all, is the medium-term impact of market integration on employment. With its injection of inflation-free growth, coupled with a loosening of the constraints on public exchequers in the Community's member states, the European home market of the 1990s raises the prospect, for the first time since the early 1970s, of very substantial job creation. The added financial elbow-room given to governments should, in addition, enable any unevenness in the rewards distributed by market integration to be compensated.[3]

This medium-term prospect of substantial growth is not just a boon for Europe. The world economy of the late 1980s and early 1990s, overshadowed by American deficits, a fickle dollar and the spectre of a US recession, needs to take confidence where it can. The expectation may be that a dynamic European market, trading with the world on a footing of revamped competitivity, will provide a much-needed shot in the arm for other markets and economies in less buoyant shape.

In return, EC governments will have the right to expect

appropriate responses from the Community's economic partners abroad, notably the US and Japan. If the fruits of the European home market are to be shared internationally, there must also be a fair share-out of the burdens of global economic responsibility, with market opening measures extended internationally on a firm basis of clear reciprocity.

The actors and the opportunity

The European home market will not materialize at the wave of a wand. 1992 will not come by whispering words of mysterious Eurospeak into a receding future, or the future will return the compliment by staying conveniently out of reach. For business and government, the two main actors, the road to market integration will be paved with tough adjustments and the need for new strategies.

For business, removing protective barriers creates a permanent opportunity, but signals a definitive end to national soft options. Cost reductions will be good news, but market opening means also the permanent threat, actual or potential, of competition. This is also good news for the company which is gearing up to capitalize on the enlarged market's enhanced opportunities for innovation and economies of scale. But profits which derive from cashing in on monopoly or protected positions will tend to be squeezed. The situation will be one of constant competitive renewal.

Managing change will mean changing management – or rather the focus of its business strategy. There is already widespread evidence that this is happening, as companies – ahead of 1992 and often way ahead of the politicians – are adjusting both their management goals and business structures in readiness for new patterns of competition. But opportunities must continue to be seized – merely to neglect them will create a threat. One thing is certain. Firms from outside the EC, who are already positioning themselves in Community markets in anticipation of the White Paper programme's success, will not miss opportunities overlooked by their indigenous rivals.

Governments, already being watched closely by business, will be expected to give clear signs of their commitment to the 1992 goal. The credibility of the European market as an operational environment for business depends in the first instance on the legislator persuading companies of the seriousness of its intentions. There is only one way of doing this. EC governments must enact the White Paper programme fully and on schedule. In so doing, they will release the costs, outlined in this book, which presently inhibit Europe's market and economic expansion.

This means a further role for companies. Business cannot afford to sit passively by, idly expecting governments to keep to long-term legislative commitments, unaided. There is a need of more active political involvement, in the sense of constructive input to policy, orchestrated at Community level but targetted above all at the seats of national political power.

But governments must do more than achieve the European home market. They must maintain it – and, once again, give companies tangible proof that they are committed to doing so.

No great insight is needed to see that maintaining market integration will in turn pose the Community with some ineluctable choices. The business managers of the European market of the 1990s cannot be indefinitely divorced from the political managers of the Community economy.

Attempting to sustain this unserviceable dichotomy would be to invite disaster. Market integration, for example, particularly in its early stages, is likely to accentuate pressures on exchange rates and thus the need for firm currency management and for a stronger European monetary system. Without an institutional framework to deal effectively with these and other problems inherent in the success of the 1992 programme, the European home market will soon be put in jeopardy. The tensions that will be created will not be susceptible of management in an institutional vacuum. In short, for Europe to meet its market challenge, it must also, sooner rather than later, review the overall structure of its economic organisation.

PART I
EUROPE'S FRAGMENTED MARKETS – THE COST FACTOR

1 The uncommon market: 'Integration' – 20 years on

Many will remember the Common Market.

Not perhaps as a fact, because despite much noteworthy effort and several false dawns it has never really materialized. But as an ambition which, it was generally assumed, had been substantially fulfilled by events like the removal of import tariffs between European Community countries at the end of the 1960s, and the programme for removing intra-EC technical barriers launched in 1969.

By the mid-1980s, the error of this assumption, which business had experienced for some time, was beginning to dawn on the Community's political leaders. 'Common Market' became a term used with growing embarrassment and decreasing accuracy to describe the trading and market relationship between EC member countries. Events since then are well-known. In 1985 the EC summit endorsed the European Commission's *White Paper on Completing the internal market*.[4] This set out a detailed legislative programme for creating real home market conditions in Europe by 1992 via some 300 acts to remove non-tariff barriers. By early 1988, with a third of the journey to 1992 over, just under a quarter have been adopted.

What remains is a daunting, uphill task given the scale of the problem. Because today's Common Market, just to give a few random examples, is still one where:

- customs-related costs put a charge on companies equal to a major portion of their profits from intra-EC trade; firms in effect pay a penalty dividend (around 25% of profits in many sectors) to national border controllers for the privilege of going European;
- industry in areas like motor manufacturing and telecommunications is losing billions of Ecus because of inefficiencies imposed by divergent product standards or protectionist procurement;
- smaller companies are to a significant extent debarred from transborder business activity by administrative costs and regulatory hassles;
- a bewildering array of price differences faces consumers of essential services: car insurance may vary by as much as 300% between high and low price countries; tariffs for telephone

services can vary 50% from one EC country to another; the range of price differences for some key financial services can be even greater;

- the public authorities, year in year out, pay around Ecu 17,500m more than they should in purchasing the goods and services they need – because of protective procurement systems over which they themselves preside.

This is just a smattering of the evidence, outlined in greater detail in the following pages, as to the cost of the barriers which still fragment the EC market – the 'costs of non-Europe'.

Barriers that have to go

The basic finding, corroborating that of the White Paper, is that a whole series of barriers will have to go if European companies, consumers and governments are to be freed from these costs and enjoy a real European home market in the 1990s. They fall into three broad types:

- *physical barriers* – like intra-EC border stoppages, customs controls and associated paperwork;
- *technical barriers* – for example, meeting divergent national product standards, technical regulations and conflicting business laws; entering nationally protected public procurement markets;
- *fiscal barriers* – especially differing rates of VAT and excise duties.

Getting an accurate feel for which are the worst barriers is difficult, but business in the manufacturing sector has supplied its own verdict. A survey specially commissioned for the research involving 11,000 businessmen, showed that administrative and customs barriers, coupled with divergent national standards and regulations, are top of the aggravation list (see Table 1.1. below).

Calculating the costs of Europe's fragmented market

Of course, these barriers impact with greater or less severity depending on the sector. Similarly, the costs linked to them vary from one business to another. Thus, manufacturing companies, it emerges, are typically worst hit by customs formalities, technical regulations and disparate tax treatment. In areas like telecommunications, energy and transport, protectionist public procurement policies tend to sustain high prices and/or inefficient companies. The service sectors appear worst hit by specific market regulations which impede competition, for example, in insurance, banking and air and truck transport. Without necessarily intending to do so, these rules

4

Table 1.1 *Ranking of market barriers by business**

Total industry	B	DK	D	GR	E	F	IRL	I	L	NL	P	UK	EUR 12
1) National standards and regulations	2	1	1	7	6	1	2	4	2	3	4	1	2
2) Government procurement	6	8	8	8	8	7/8	7	2	8	7	3	4	8
3) Administrative barriers	1	2	2	1	1	2	1	1	1	1	1	2	1
4) Physical frontier delays and costs	3	3	4	3	2	4	3	3	3	2	2	3	3
5) Differences in VAT	8	7	5/6	4/5	7	3	6	7	7	8	8	8	6/7
6) Regulations of freight transport	5	4/5	5/6	4/5	3	5	4	8	5	4	5	5	6/7
7) Restrictions in capital market	4	6	7	2	5	7/8	5	5	4	6	6	7	5
8) Community law	7	4/5	3	6	4	6	8	6	6	5	7	6	4

Ranks are based on the answers to the question: 'How important do you consider this barrier to be removed?' Range of ranks:: 1 (most important) to 8 (least important).

B = Belgium	GR = Greece	IRL = Ireland	NL = Netherlands
DK = Denmark	E = Spain	I = Italy	P = Portugal
D = Germany	F = France	L = Luxemburg	UK = United Kingdom

* Source: Survey of the EC Commission (Nerb, forthcoming)

restrict entry to services' markets at least as severely as differing technical specifications do for manufacturing firms, and often more so.

A more detailed estimation of the costs of Europe's fragmented markets is outlined in Chapters 2–7. Their source is the research set out in the thirteen basic reports undertaken for the cost of non-Europe research programme (see diagram below). They look respectively at the costs of some major barriers which affect all business and then at the specific cost impact on selected service and manufacturing sectors.

Thus Chapters 2–5 examine consecutively the costs of

- red tape and delays created by customs formalities
- restrictive practices in public procurement
- the maze of divergent product standards
- conflicting business and tax regulations hindering transborder business activity.

The last two chapters of Part I then look more specifically at the costs of market fragmentation. Their impact on Europe's service economy (financial, business and telecom services) is considered in Chapter 6, while Chapter 7 probes the cost of non-Europe for selected manufacturing industries (telecom equipment, motor manufacturing, foodstuffs, building materials, textiles and clothing, and pharmaceuticals).

Taken together, these chapters summarize the first coherent attempt at a general insight into the malfunctionings of the Community market – or the workings of non-Europe. Inevitably, in view of the magnitude and novelty of the task, the results of the research are bounded with a degree of caution, but the composite picture of unnecessary costs and lost opportunities is unmistakable. It is put in overall perspective by the general economic estimates of the benefits accruing to the European economy to be found in Part II. But already in Part I the picture is one of debilitating costs which, if not crippling European businesses at home, ensure that they step out to confront global competition with lead weights round both feet.

EC market fragmentation: the 13 reports

The costs of non-Europe are analysed in 13 reports* dealing with:

– multi-sectoral barriers:
- Customs formalities, including delays imposed on road haulage
- Public procurement procedures
- Technical regulations and product standards
- Impediments to cross-frontier business link-ups

– service sector:
- business services
- financial services
- telecom services

– manufacturing sectors:
- telecom equipment
- automobiles
- foodstuffs
- building materials
- textile and clothing
- pharmaceuticals

* References to research in the text refer to the above reports except where specified.

2 Red-tape and border-related controls – bad for business, worst for small firms

The most obstructive barriers to cross-border trade, in the view of business itself, are administrative formalities and the border controls to which they are so often linked. This emerges clearly from the business survey[5] in which company executives pinpoint paperwork, red tape and frontier checks as high on the list of obstacles hampering the dispatch of goods to other Community markets. Not all of these barriers are experienced at national borders, but it is to them that they trace their roots, and it is they that epitomize best the psychological as well as material reality of non-Europe.

Business, of course, is not the only victim of border formalities. Consumers very often have to dig deeper into their pockets for goods produced across the border. And the individual traveller has his own tale to tell, often of experiences verging on the feudal. People travelling as if they were in a real common market can be painfully reminded of their false assumptions, and the Commission has had to intervene in a series of cases where it appeared that arbitrary penalties were meted out for petty documentary errors:

- a lorry driver, given incorrect documents from a customs agent in Dover, was fined FF 60,000;
- a German employee going on a course in the company's French subsidiary had his personal computer confiscated and was fined before the Commission intervened;
- a tourist carrying personal goods declared as a gift was fined DR 300,000 at Greek customs.

But it is companies which appear to face the costliest problems. These are quantified by the research on customs formalities which was itself based on interviews with around 500 firms in six EC countries (Belgium, France, Germany, Italy, the Netherlands and the United Kingdom). The essence of the story is quickly told (see Table 2.1). EC-wide, firms pay around Ecu 8 billion in administrative costs and delays occasioned by intra-EC customs procedures – or getting on for 2% of these transborder sales. Moreover, the turnover companies forego as a result is at least Ecu 4.5 billion and possibly as

Table 2.1   Administrative formalities and border controls – the bill

Ecu millions	Costs
7,500	administration
415-830	delays
4,500-15,000	business foregone
500-1,000	government spending* on intra-EC customs controls

*On 6-country basis: Belgium, France, Germany, Italy, the Netherlands, UK.

high as Ecu 15 billion. Governments get off more lightly, spending some Ecu 500m-1000m of taxpayers' money on the human resources required to artificially restrict trade. This of course takes no account of the profit taxes they forego on the company sales they have thus inhibited.

The direct costs to companies of intra-EC customs formalities emerge from an empirical analysis, conducted in the research, of the impact of these procedures on transborder consignments made by the firms surveyed. It was found that the average cost of these form-filling checks – occasioned by VAT and excise payments, health and veterinary controls etc. (see diagram below) – was around Ecu 67-86 per consignment at both its export and import phase: in other words, a total of Ecu 153, or around 1.5% of the average consignment's value. When costs of delays are added to this, a figure nearer to 2% is reached. For businessmen with single-digit profit margins, its removal might be viewed as a welcome source of increased flexibility.

The smaller you are the more you pay
Things are even worse for small or middle-sized companies – the very type of firm on which the Community's political leaders have lavished repeated words of encouragement in recent years. Customs costs per consignment, according to the research findings, can be up to 30% to 45% higher for companies with under 250 employees than for larger companies. Words of political support, while welcome, are not as beneficial to these firms as action to abolish the cost of customs administration.

Such action, including the introduction of simplified customs procedures, has begun to be taken by the EC. Three measures were implemented on 1 January 1988 which, over time, should make life easier for companies engaged in trade across EC borders, namely:

• a harmonized system of commodity description and coding;

9

- the new Community tariff (TARIC) applying to goods whose description is harmonized in this way;
- the single administrative document – a new trading form, replacing an array of others, to be used for the export, import and transit of goods over Community frontiers.

Larger enterprises, it seems, are adapting better to living with cumbersome border formalities. This is borne out again by the business survey. Big business, which accounts for the bulk of intra-Community trade, has the size to make the management adjustments to benefit from simplified procedures, enabling it to avoid the worst inroads of border raids into corporate administration. But there's no getting away from the basic fact. The smaller you are, the greater the cost of customs-related paperwork, the more you pay – and the more you stand to gain by moves to eliminate customs controls.

Geographical divides

The big/small divide isn't the only unevenness in the impact of the cost of EC frontier checks. There are also some startling geographical discrepancies, as shown by a sample of the results thrown up by the research (see Table 2.2).

From the standpoint of the cost of border hassles, the message for companies appears clear. The market of the Benelux countries – the Belgo-Luxembourg economic union and the Netherlands – is a good place to do business. There the costs are lower than for trade

Table 2.2 *Average costs per consignment in intra-EC trade (ECU)*

Country	Imports	Exports
Belgium	26	34
France	92	87
Germany	.42	79
Italy	130	205
Netherlands	46	50
United Kingdom	75	49

between Benelux countries and other EC countries, and than for other EC countries between themselves. And trade between Italy and other countries, according to these figures, is more costly than between any other country and the rest of the Community.

At opposite extremes of the sample are respectively Belgium and Italy. In the former, apparently thanks to the simplified documentation procedures within the Benelux customs union, there are markedly lower customs clearance costs than the average. A special plaudit goes to the 'Benelux 50' document which effectively facilitates trade between Benelux countries by providing all the necessary information for VAT and customs statistics purposes.

By contrast, the costs of importing into Italy are, at Ecu 130 per consignment, precisely five times higher than the estimated import charge into Belgium. The high costs found in Italy do not come as a total surprise – certainly not to anyone who has pondered the value of the control of the huge queues of trucks building back from the Italian and Alpine frontiers. They have been prefigured by business representations made to the Commission complaining, in particular, at the existence of two customs administrations at Italian borders effectively carrying out the same checks. The problems caused by this double control are further compounded by uncertainties for companies caused by Italian sanitary controls.

The worst situation appears to be the one suffered by a small or medium-sized company in Italy seeking to develop markets elsewhere in the Community: it is likely, because of the special problems facing smaller business, to face an export deterrent even larger than the one indicated in Table 2.2 Inversely, smaller firms elsewhere seeking to develop the Italian market are not much better off.

Calculating, from the evidence in the report, the overall customs-related administrative costs borne by Community business, a round figure of Ecu 7.5 billion is reached. To this a further irritant must be added. This is a net charge of at least Ecu 415m and at most 830m ascribable to the physical delays at borders imposed on Europe's road haulage business. This estimate, it should be emphasized, takes no account of the cost of delays faced by inland water and rail transport.

Transborder road transport: a long haul made longer

The problems facing international road haulage operators in Europe, as a result of the fragmented Community market, are manifold, among them: delays at frontier posts and enforced empty truck movements linked to restrictions like national permit quotas and those on 'cabotage' (meaning collection and delivery limits on non-resident hauliers). In addition, beyond these economic costs are the psychological stresses caused for drivers by unnecessary delays.

The Ecu 415m-830m spread in the cost of delays facing hauliers at customs posts reflects a number of factors. The upper limit represents the total estimated costs of delay. But delay time is not necessarily effective time lost, since it is assumed, for instance, that hauliers plan to make compulsory driver rest times coincide with delays at customs points. Allowing generously for this results in the lower, Ecu 415m, figure for costs.

The impact of these delays on average haulier costs is difficult to quantify. But illustrative of their dimension is the example reported of the comparative experience of two 1200 km truck trips – one within the UK and one from London to Milan. The first took 36 hours. The second (excluding time lost in the Channel crossing) took 58 hours. This example[6] suggests that frontier delays between the UK and Italy amount to a crude increase in transport costs as between these two markets of over 50%.

This is not all. Beyond delay costs are those related to the permit and cabotage restrictions which, from a regulatory standpoint, make the road haulage sector one of the most illiberal in Europe. Putting an authoritative number on these latter costs is also difficult. However, what does emerge is the existence of much under-utilized capacity in the form of part-loaded lorries, an important element of which at least is attributable to commercial restrictions. With the cost of such inefficiencies often being passed on, it is the Community's manufacturing industry that foots much of the bill for the regulations in which the European transport sector has been traditionally strait-jacketed.

American experience

The costs of a highly-regulated trucking sector – and the benefits of removing them – are further underscored by experience in the US which, until a recent reform, was also characterized by high transport rates often supported by restrictive practices at state-level. By comparison with the EC, the American system now provides several competitive advantages to its industry, including:

- no authorization for interstate trucking;
- differences in state taxation and regulations not so great as to distort hauliers' operating costs anything like as much as in the EC (see also diagram below).

Following the Motor Carrier Reform Act of 1980, which essentially did away with the state-based restrictive practices, the charge of transport inefficiencies on overall American economic welfare appears to have been significantly reduced. The benefit from transport deregulation is estimated in the region of US$ 26 billion.

Road haulage liberalization in the US

The following benefits have appeared in recent years in the more deregulated American states:

- increased competition has lowered freight rates and improved the level and choice of services;
- hauliers have given new resources to marketing, planning and innovation;
- the total number of carriers has increased, despite bankruptcies affecting big and small alike;
- smaller hauliers have survived, mainly by occupying niche markets.

Lost market opportunities and turnover

Beyond the direct costs they impose on companies, customs formalities and delays also lead to business foregoing opportunities which otherwise are there for the taking. This cost in lost intra-EC trade, according to the research, is estimated at between Ecu 4.5 billion and Ecu 15 billion for business in the Community as a whole. Unsurprisingly, it is smaller business which feels it suffers most from lost sales potential.

A case in point concerns the mail order business. Because of the administrative costs involved, companies which cannot immediately achieve an Ecu 1 million cross-border turnover are in a no-go situation, and even those who manage this must quintuple sales rapidly if they are to keep on the business. Most smaller companies throw in the sponge well before this.[7]

The big spread in the above general estimate for lost trade (representing between 1% and 3% of intra-Community trade of Ecu 500 billion) reflects the differing expectations of respectively the importers and exporters surveyed. Exporters expect gains three times as great as importers from the removal of customs checks. This seems to show considerably more enthusiasm from the export trade for what, when it occurs, will of course be a balanced situation.

There are also big differences between the evaluations made by small and big business about the lost sales potential attributable to customs compliance procedures. For both imports and exports, smaller firms look forward to increases the double of those foreseen by their larger brethren. Thus, of the companies surveyed who responded expecting trade increases from the removal of border controls, those with less than 50 employees expected average increases in exports of 26% and in imports of 22%, while the expectations of those with more than 500 staff were for 10% export and 8% import growth. (The final weighted overall figures are much smaller since they take account of companies which forecast no change in the present situation.)

The estimate of trade foregone because of customs barriers needs to be put in a broader perspective. It is important to remember that even the Ecu 15 billion figure (3% of intra-EC trade) is some way below the overall trade gains which company executives expect from the removal of all trade barriers (ie not just customs formalities). These, according to the 11,000 executives replying to the general business survey, amount to an average in the region of 5% of their trading figure.

Public expenditure

European governments, who have it in their collective power to promote business by removing these barriers, also bear a share of the direct costs of the system over which they preside. For even the administration required to keep trade barriers in place has its cost to the public purse. Government expenditure earmarked for this purpose is estimated by the research at between a further Ecu 500m and Ecu 1000m.

This estimate, based on an analysis of six EC countries (Belgium, France, Germany, Italy, Netherlands and the UK), corresponds to between 15,000 and 30,000 staff who are involved in the administration of intra-EC customs and tax controls. The assessment takes account of a variety of factors, eg the staff still required for national controls and for non-EC international trade etc. The upper figure, of 30,000, should be seen against the 75,000 currently employed in the national customs administrations of the six countries surveyed. In other words, the research does not posit the sudden miraculous disappearance in 1992 of all customs officials, but rather the reallocation of those involved in formalities which are counterproductive to the functioning of a single European market thereafter.

Policy responses in the White Paper

As regards the larger picture of trade costs, EC governments have begun to take some of the measures needed to reduce border checks. The introduction on 1 January 1988 of the single administrative document (Sad) and other customs measures (see above p.9–10) seeks to curtail some of the demands of paperwork on EC cross-border traders.

Other measures recently taken by the Community include the agreement, reached in principle in June 1986, to move towards the phased liberalization of road haulage permits and a quota-free Europe in 1992. This decision, which is since proving difficult to implement, provides for 40% annual increases in the number of Community-wide permits. By 1992 it should be clear whether the positive impact of this move has been proportionately as great as that apparently achieved by the process of American deregulation begun in the early 1980s (see p.12–13).

The full programme for deregulating the cross-border movement of goods is spelt out for governments in the White Paper's legislative programme for 1992. The drag on company sales and profits constituted by border controls would, for all practical purposes, be eliminated if they adopted the various proposals in the White Paper dealing with health and veterinary controls, VAT and excise harmonization, the removal of residual national quotas on items like textiles and automobiles etc. – in short, if they eliminated all internal borders. Equally, until governments grasp this nettle, businessmen may continue to perceive transborder trade as much a source of costs as an area of opportunity. Downstream of the businessman, the consumer is arguably even worse off. For him, customs procedures represent perhaps the most explicit and symbolic of barriers supporting non-competitive business practices for which, in the last analysis, he pays.

3   Government protectionism in procurement markets – a shot in the foot

Cross-frontier trade between private-sector business in the EC has, despite the many residual obstacles, developed strongly in the 30 years since the Community's formation in 1958. Not so the public sector, whose purchasing programmes, in the vast majority of cases, stop still at national borders.

Yet there can be no doubt about the importance to the EC economy of public procurement, about the potential benefits to competitive business and the consumer if it were more open, and the costs currently incurred because it is not.

Take its size, for a start. In 1986 total purchasing controlled by the public sector (central and local government, their agencies, and enterprises with monopoly-type concessions) was worth Ecu 530 billion (larger incidentally than the ECU 500 billion for intra-EC trade). This amounts to 15% of the Community's gross domestic product. Of course a hefty portion of the overall figure is earmarked for goods and services which are inherently non-competitive, non-tradable or are required in quantities too small to come within contractual procedures. All the same, the residue for contractual procurement, or public markets, is estimated at a sizeable Ecu 240–340 billion (equal to between 7% and 10% of Gdp). But only a fraction of this smaller total (an infinitessimal 0.14% of Gdp) is awarded to companies from other EC countries.

There are, of course, some good reasons for buying locally – eg. lower transport and trading costs, more efficient after-sales service, and quicker delivery. However, these should not be exaggerated nor disguise the built-in reluctance of purchasers to tender to non-national suppliers.

The costs of almost hermetically-sealed procurement practices are major and various. By not encouraging intra-EC competition – if not by deliberately rejecting it – the public sector pays more than it should for the goods it needs and, in so doing, supports sub-optimal enterprises in the Community. Certain high technology areas of telecoms, power generation, railways and defence are characterized by dominant public buyers, very few suppliers and little intra-EC trade. Market fragmentation makes European industry in these areas less competitive in world markets than it otherwise might be – and has to be to survive with Japan and the USA in the global markets of the 1990s. Protectionist support, often portrayed as a shot in the arm for industry, is in fact a striking example of governments shooting themselves, and their competitive ideals, in the foot. Indeed, the European public sector shows substantially the opposite behaviour, in the conduct of its own business affairs, to that which its leaders in government are repeatedly urging companies to adopt in the economy at large.

Three major areas for cost savings

In money terms, the potential public expenditure savings gained by removing these inefficiencies are, according to the research in this area, estimated in a spread of Ecu 8–19 billion for the five countries surveyed (Belgium, France, Germany, Italy and the UK in 1984). These savings stem from the realization of three beneficial effects which will occur, according to the report, consecutively:

- the 'static trade effect' – meaning public authorities buying from the cheapest (ie foreign) suppliers (Ecu 3–8 billion);
- the 'competition effect', leading to downward pressure on prices charged by domestic firms in previously closed sectors, as they strive to compete with foreign companies entering the market (Ecu 1–3 billion);
- the 'restructuring effect', or the longer-run effect of economies of scale, occurring as industry reorganizes under the pressure of new competitive conditions (Ecu 4–8 billion). This saving is concentrated in certain high tech sectors like computers, telecoms, aerospace.

But this is not the limit of potential benefits. Further items, but which are impossible to quantify, include:

- savings for private sector buyers who pay less for goods (eg. office equipment, building materials) whose prices have been reduced by the break-up of restrictive trade practices in the public sector;
- the dynamic effects of greater competition on innovation, investment and growth.

Adjusting the figures upwards for the twelve EC countries, and averaging out the spread, total savings estimated at around Ecu 17.5 billion (or 0.5% of 1986 Community Gdp) would result from open public procurement Community-wide. In addition, if defence procurement is included (an area not covered by the research programme) separate estimates[8] suggest that gains of another Ecu 4 billion could be achieved by market opening in this sector. On this basis, the total cost of non-Europe in public procurement would amount to Ecu 21.5 billion.

Parts of the story behind these figures are illustrated later in this chapter by reference to sectors like telecoms, power turbines and data-processing. Suffice it to recall here the key conclusion reached, namely that around half of the estimated potential savings are concentrated in these sectors, and that, as the report puts it: 'unless restrictions on public purchasing are swept away, far from strategic industries being protected, whole areas of industry which have high multiplier effects on other sectors of manufacturing could cease to be viable'.

Legislation no match for protectionist bureaucracies

In public procurement, the divide between economic reality and political appearances is so deep as to be almost hallucinatory. On the one hand, as shown above, there is the huge implicit cost of minimal import penetration caused by national procurement protection. On the other, there is EC legislation, enacted in the 1970s, apparently enforcing open award procedures for procurement. The false optimism created by Community directives on public works (1971) and public supply contracts (1977) is further indulged by the facile assurances of the authorities themselves. 'Public purchasing authorities', say the authors of the research report, 'generally deny that overt nationalistic purchasing policies exist'.

Several factors explain the gap between liberal appearance and protectionist reality. First, Community legislation on public purchasing has so far excluded sectors characterized by nationalistic procurement for strategic reasons – and where there are in some cases large specialist contracts of interest for foreign suppliers. These sectors are:

- energy
- transport
- telecommunications
- water supply

However, the problem runs much deeper than this. Sectoral exceptions are one thing, but more alarming is that EC rules on awarding procedures have had very little effect in the areas of procurement actually within their scope. The stark fact is that the Community legislator has up to now proved no match for national and local purchasing bureaucracies.

Legislation on procurement has not had much direct effect on trade because, among other reasons :

- there are too many ways to evade the rules or influence the choice of supplier during the evaluation of bids;
- other barriers to trade (like divergent national standards) still exist and these lead to price differences, distorting competitive bidding;
- in many countries, purchasing is significantly decentralized, making EC transparency rules hard to enforce.

Reasons for protection
Avoidance of competition of course has its rationale. Public procurement is typically used by EC member states, to support national and regional firms and industries either:

- for strategic reasons (eg. defence, telecoms, aerospace)
- to support employment in declining industries
- to compensate local communities near environmentally damaging public industries (eg. coal mining, nuclear fuels)
- to support emerging high tech industries (eg. new telecom systems, lasers)
- or for more general political reasons (eg. highly visible goods like cars, tableware).

Injecting competition into public procurement – new EC proposals
Faced with the absence of competition and the limited success of Community legislation so far, the EC Commission has moved to implement the White Paper by proposing to:

- close down the loopholes in existing EC rules for public works and supply markets, thus easing market entry by non-nationals
- provide companies with legal redress to assert their rights under EC rules, and to ensure awarding authorities comply with them
- extend open awards procedures to currently excluded markets – energy, transport, telecommunications and water supply – and subsequently to bring the service sector within their ambit.

Potential price savings for specific products
In order to assess the potential price savings which would result from open competition, researchers made a series of calculations, based on tested assumptions, relating to a range of specific products in the five countries surveyed (Belgium, France, Germany, Italy and the UK). A sample of the savings to be derived from the combined impact of static and competitive effects (p.17) includes:

Pharmaceuticals: 52% price saving in Germany; 40% in the UK
Office machinery and instrumentation: 12% saving in France, 27% in Italy

Telephone switching: 60% saving (Belgium); 40% (France); 70% (Germany); 50% (Italy, the UK)

Telephones: 20% saving (Belgium); 43% (France); 39% (Germany)

Electrical equipment (weighted average): 17% saving (Belgium); 14% (France); 15% (Germany); 14% (Italy); 7% (UK)

Motor vehicles (weighted average): 13% (France); 4% (Germany); 10% (Italy); 9% (UK).

Coal: a 50% price saving in Germany; 25% in the UK

The price savings indicated above provide a broad indication of the extent to which, in the countries concerned, products are overpriced due to protection from competition. Other items for which the report identifies substantial gains (25%–50%) as a result of procurement liberalization in high price countries include X-ray machines (France, Germany, Italy), uniforms (Belgium, France, Italy) and filing cabinets (Germany). The report also finds that for several products there are no apparent potential savings at all (eg. fluorescent tubes, school desks, cement and cardiac monitors).

Particular impact of restrictions on strategic sectors

The negative consequence of closed and protective procurement is that in certain key high tech supply sectors (capital equipment for defence, power generation, telecoms and railways) where public authorities are the major purchasers, a symbiotic relationship has gradually built up between suppliers and buyers. This economic incest is a breeding ground for commercial deformities and deviant competitive behaviour. Among the barriers and distortions to intra-EC trade which such a relationship either encourages or tolerates, and whose elimination will be needed effectively to open up public procurement, are:

- widely differing national or exclusive user standards;
- government subsidies;
- R&D efforts duplicated, dispersed and sub-optimal;
- maintenance of companies with little incentive to invest in new technologies to confront competition from non-EC firms; with shortsighted marketing and production strategies unable to rival the Europe-wide strategies of US and Japanese competitors; with insufficient specialization and economies of scale.

Given this, it is no surprise that in most of the key industrial sectors the largest world firms are generally US or Japanese. They are not just more competitive than Europeans on world markets, but are better organized to compete for EC-wide markets. The fact that the Community has more companies does not do it much good. It adds nothing to the degree of competition in Community countries, because the protectiveness of European national markets merely sustains their sub-optimal performance.

Economies of scale – gearing up for global rivalry
At present in many key sectors, companies are operating without the specialization and size necessary to compete globally. An important contributory cause of this is the protection afforded by closed procurement.

The research looks at the gains in product costs and customer prices which would result in selected sectors from economies of scale triggered by more open competition. Sectors analysed in case studies conducted by the research include those which, together with some of their main characteristics, are outlined in the following table. Generally speaking these industries suffer excess capacity, except telephones and mainframe computers. There is also virtually nil intra-EC trade, except for mainframe computers (mainly due to IBM, according to the report) and public switching equipment (mainly due to trade between local European subsidiaries).

Table 3.1   Main characteristics of some key markets

Product	Approx EC market m ECUs	Estimated capacity utilization	Significance of intra-EC trade
Boilers	2,000	20%	negl
Turbine Generators	2,000	60%	negl
Locomotives	100	50%–80%	negl
Mainframe computers	10,000	80%	medium to great
Public Switching	7,000	approx 70%	medium
Telephones	5,000	90%	negl

There follows in very abbreviated form the developments which the report expects for these sectors in a Europe-wide competitive environment, including the price advantages resulting from economies of scale in the short and longer-run.

Boilers
There is no trade between EC producing countries, and there is massive overcapacity. Increased competition in the Community's

21

internal market would lead to some loss in boilermaking capacity, reducing the number of firms from 15 (in the five countries surveyed) to around four. Unit prices and costs would fall by around 20%. Changes in national competition policy would be needed as well as opening up procurement.

Turbine generators
There is little trade, and also some overcapacity. Italy and the UK are beginning new power station building programmes, so French and German firms would be able to enter these markets. This is likely to lead to mergers and acquisitions and rationalization of production, reducing unit costs by an estimated 12%, without major closures.

Electric locomotives
Merger and collaboration agreements are just beginning to occur in a sector traditionally characterized by negligible trade. Purchasing is opening up, but its impact on intra-EC trade will only slowly follow. Over a period of decades, the number of main manufacturers is likely to reduce from 16 to about three or four. Unit costs would fall by around 13%. Pressure for these changes already exists because of changing technology, but they cannot occur without changes in public purchasing policy.

Mainframe computers
Unlike the three above sectors, this is already a highly competitive industry, even if it is largely characterized by indigenous producers competing against IBM in each national market. Some continued rationalization of the industry is likely, leading to minor savings in R&D and marketing, probably worth around 5% of costs. Europe, however, now has fewer manufacturers (5 including IBM) than the USA (9 firms).

Public exchange switching equipment
There are seven different digital switching systems being installed in EC countries, five of which were developed by EC firms with the protection of national purchasing policies and R&D funding. In 1987, the price per line was reported as ranging in the EC between $225 and $500, compared to around $100 in the US. With open tendering the European price would probably fall to around $150. Industry has been restructuring rapidly recently to compete for national market shares, notably by the emergence of Alcatel as a major pan-European firm. With completely open markets there would probably be only two firms in the EC in the longer-run.

Telephones

There are many manufacturers of telephones and significant imports into deregulated markets (in particular the UK). There are substantial price differences, mainly reflecting the high specifications for telephones into regulated markets and less sophisticated products in free markets. Free competition would drive out expensive products and high cost producers, bringing prices down by 30–40% in France and Germany.

4 Divergences in technical regulations and standards – costs difficult to quantify but impossible to ignore

Rated by companies themselves as one of most acute problems they face in their European operations (see Table 1.1), disparities between national technical regulations and standards are a complex and, to the outside observer, an arcane subject. Yet their adverse impact on industry seeking to exploit the full dimension of the EC market, a priority matter for the Community policy-maker as for the businessman, is now widely accepted.

It is not difficult to see why. In an increasing number of sectors, firms will be obliged to survive by selling in quantities much larger than are likely to be absorbed by their share of a single, narrow national market. To compete, they need to produce on a larger scale. To amortize this investment in new plant, and also their spiralling expenditure on research and innovation, they need the larger, European market.

National product regulations and standards, however, impose an entirely contrary logic. They tend, by their differences, to force companies to do what their business strategy tells them is wrong: produce for the national market, innovate for the national market. Manufacturers are thus often constrained either to limit themselves to a sub-optimal market, or to attack new markets via a range of sub-optimal plants and narrowly relevant technology. Either option implies extensive costs – the costs of non-Europe.

Adverse effects are thus not limited to restrictions on cross-border trade. They impact on the core functions of business – production and technology. And the costs they incur are often compounded by their use in combination with other obstacles to market entry, notably restrictive public procurement, eg. telecommunications equipment (Chapter 7). Among the worst affected by these and related barriers are high tech sectors which are precisely those where market fragmentation has a proven track record in putting Europe at a competitive disadvantage with the US and Japan.

Barriers in this field result from differences between EC countries for three types of arrangement: technical regulations, standards, testing and certification procedures.

Technical regulations lay down legal requirements, enacted by the national legislator mainly in the interests of health, safety and the environment; often these requirements refer to standards.

Standards are not legally binding in themselves, since they are written by private national standardisation bodies like DIN (in Germany), BSI (in Britain) and AFNOR (in France). However, although standards are only voluntary codifications for products and product processes, they often assume a quasi-legal status because of their use as a reference in technical regulations and, for example, in insurance and product liability claims, as well as in calls for tender for public procurement.

Testing and certification procedures are used to check that a product or process complies either with voluntary standards or with statutory regulations. If successfully passed, they result in the issuance of certificates of conformity. However, a typical problem is non-recognition by one EC country of another's certification process, meaning at best additional testing and at worst an absolute market entry barrier.

Costs: multi-sector impact
The costs (see diagram below) imposed by these barriers hit manufacturing industries right across the board. But they do so in a manner which is so sector-specific and which, even then, is often inextricably combined with the impact of other barriers, as to make a quantified extrapolation at the general level impossible to undertake. But on an individual industry basis, the story is clear. It is illustrated by the investigations carried out by the research into certain selected industries (see Chapter 7). Their results are in turn corroborated and amplified by company executives themselves in the general survey of manufacturing business conducted for the research.[9]

Telecom equipment, automobiles, foodstuffs, pharmaceuticals and the building products sector are, as shown in Chapter 7, five major EC industries where standards and technical regulations, alone or in combination with other obstacles, inject heavy doses of inefficiency into business operations.

This is most spectacularly the case in the telecom sector. Here the industry's regulators – usually the national PTTs – have traditionally sustained their restrictive procurement practices by demanding observance of narrowly relevant standards reinforced by discriminating certification procedures. The overall cost of these mutually supportive barriers is estimated as high as Ecu 4.8 billion.

25

The experience of telecom equipment, moreover, is to an extent indicative of the massive losses imposed by divergent standards on other high technology sectors, where burgeoning R&D expenditure can only be recouped by manufacturing products to widely marketable standards.

At the other end of industry's product range, foodstuffs and building products have their own experiences to tell. Thus of the total estimated costs of up to Ecu 1 billion attributable to market barriers in the foodstuffs sector, content and ingredient regulations on just four items (chocolates, beer, ice-cream and pasta) contribute over 80% (see Chart 7.1). In the building products sector, research shows unequivocally that divergent standards and lengthy certification (whose procedures can last years rather than months) are the primary causes of non-Europe costs estimated in total at around Ecu 2.5 billion. Pharmaceutical companies, meanwhile, face serious problems and significant costs in getting new products authorized and admitted to the market.

Motor manufacturing enjoys a paradoxical but costly situation. It is both the sector where the removal of technical barriers is judged as most necessary by business itself (see Table 1.1) and yet the one where the Community has had most apparent success in harmonizing technical regulations. As many as 41 EC harmonization directives, dealing with specifications for various parts of the automobile, have been adopted over the years. But the key problem is that there remain three further directives which need to be adopted before full EC type approval can be achieved. In the absence of Community type approval (which is being held up on political rather than technical grounds), and thus of a European certification procedure, EC-wide manufacturers are generally being forced into costly duplications.

Product development in the auto sector
– the supplementary EC Bill

- No less than Ecu 286m is estimated as the extra bill imposed by divergent European specifications etc. on the product development costs of a volume passenger car, according to a recent study*;
- Included in this is the cost of meeting differing require- ments for engineering, production, product planning, type- approval, certification etc.

*A report by the Motor Industry Research Unit Ltd commissioned by Ford of Europe

The businessmen's verdict
The business survey commissioned for the 'non-Europe' research programme bears out and supplements these sectoral findings. It elicited answers from 11,000 business respondents throughout the EC who were asked how important they considered the removal of technical trade barriers to be for their company. After weighting the responses, the results of the survey, shown abridged in tabular form below, indicate the gravity with which technical regulations and standards are considered to impact on various manufacturing sectors.

Table 4.1   Rank (top ten) in descending order of importance of technical trade barriers[10]

1. Motor vehicles	6. Other transport equipment
2. Electrical engineering	7. Food and tobacco
3. Mechanical engineering	8. Leather
4. Pharmaceuticals (and some chemicals)	9. Precision & medical equipment
5. Non-metallic mineral products	10. Metal articles

The survey shows that investment goods are viewed as suffering more than consumer products from divergent technical trade barriers. The table's hierarchy also reinforces some of the principal conclusions of the sectoral research. The electrical engineering sector, for example, suffers directly from the differing standards affecting telecom equipment and other high technology areas.

An outstanding example of the impact on investment goods of differing regulations, particularly regarding safety, is the mechanical engineering industry. A proposal made by the Commission in 1987 seeks to harmonize the safety and other essential requirements which affect many companies in the engineering machinery market, whose total annual turnover is estimated at around Ecu 200 billion.

New policy responses
The problems created for manufacturing industry by divergent technical regulations and standards pose a special challenge for the European Community. A feel for its scope was provided back in 1983[11] by the estimate of some 100,000 different specifications operating across industry. But the challenge has intensified as new regulatory and standardization initiatives have multiplied. This has essentially been in response to two pressures – adapting to technical progress, and to increased concern for health, safety and the environment.

To meet this challenge, the EC has developed in recent years a new, three-pronged approach whose interlocking components, described below, are expressed by the following key terms:

• mutual recognition
• selective harmonization
• mutual information procedures

Mutual recognition
The aim here is to ensure that business avails itself of its basic right to trade within the Community. The objective has been supported by a series of seminal judgments by the Court of Justice, which has emphasized that Community law does not merely prohibit barriers to intra-EC trade, but positively requires the mutual acceptance of the goods of one member country by another. In other words, the presumption is that goods lawfully produced or marketed in one member state should in principle have access to all member states. Instrumental in re-affirming this was the Court's 1979 ruling in the Cassis de Dijon case,[12] followed by a series of subsequent judgments, possibly the most celebrated of which was the ruling in 1987 on the German beer purity law (see Chapter 7, foodstuffs). The

significance of this jurisprudence in legislative terms is to reduce the scope and detail of harmonization required at the European level. However, mutual recognition is not enough by itself to solve the problem posed by technical trade barriers. This is because, in the absence of Community legislation, member states may still (on the basis of Rome Treaty Article 36) restrict trade in goods which do not respect their particular 'essential requirements' – including those for health, safety and environmental protection. As a result, exporters may be unable to trade a given product across intra-EC frontiers – either because they have failed to meet genuine essential requirements, or because they are being unlawfully obstructed by the use of essential requirements as a covert pretext to stop competitive entries to the national market. The latter case may give rise to litigation. But the former can only be solved by legislation.

Selective harmonization
Here the aim is to replace where necessary differing member state regulations on the essential requirements discussed above with harmonized Community legislation. This is one of the central thrusts of the new approach to harmonization which the EC has followed since 1985. It involves dispensing, by and large, with the traditional attempts at meticulously detailed harmonization, which were difficult to agree and often technically obsolete by the time their adoption was finally achieved.

Besides limiting the EC's legislative effort to harmonizing essential requirements, this new approach gives greater leeway to industry for choosing how it satisfies them. However, a simple and direct way of compliance is to meet the European standards now being set by the European Committee for Standardisation (CEN) and the European Committee for Electrotechnical Standardisation (CENELEC). These bodies are mandated by the EC authorities, once essential requirements have been harmonized, to develop common industrial standards applicable throughout Europe. Thus the detail of industrial specification is left for industry, acting through these channels, to determine. Acting in conjunction with the standardization process, the EC legislator limits himself to meeting the legal minimum.

This policy, as yet in its early days, is already beginning to bite. A first EC directive using the new approach was adopted in 1987 (on pressure vessels), and progress on proposals for building products, toys and industrial machinery has followed. Meanwhile, the important standards-setting role now assigned to CEN and CENELEC should alleviate the dead-weight presence of national standards in pivotal high technology areas like telecommunications and data-processing.

Mutual information procedures
Since its adoption in 1983, a Community directive has obliged member states to notify new regulations and standards to the Commission in advance of their enactment. This gives the Commission the power – so far used 30 times in response to 450 notifications – to freeze introduction of new national regulations for up to a year if it decides that a Community initiative should be undertaken. The assumption behind this initiative is that regulatory diversity in Europe can be accepted provided it does not trigger new barriers to intra-Community trade.

5 Blocks to transborder business activity – Europe's no place like home

A real home market is not just a place where companies trade without hindrance, but also one where they can operate in a cohesive regulatory environment. It is a market where the laws controlling firms and the incentives encouraging their activity are not so out of line as to make its unity a polite diplomatic fiction rather than hard economic fact – one where the rules of the game, if not the same, are not so different as to add major costs to doing business on a Europe-wide basis.

The costs facing companies linked across national boundaries within the EC, the subject of the report on transborder business activity, provide plenty of evidence of this type of obstacle facing European transnational firms. The report was based on an extensive survey of companies in France, Germany, Italy and the UK, with subsidiaries or parents in most EC countries. The obstacles highlighted by company executives interviewed included differing tax and accounting standards, divergent product norms and social security laws. These problems were analysed exclusively from the standpoint of the costs that transborder links like joint ventures or subsidiaries incurred as a result.

Costs of regulatory diversity estimated in billions
The research estimates that the charge of Europe's regulatory diversity on existing transborder operations, while difficult to quantify in detail, runs into tens of billions of Ecu. These costs are further compounded by the innumerable cases of Europe-wide business rationalization which are not even attempted because of the costs involved. The sectors surveyed in interviews with companies were in the main automobiles, machinery, textiles, telecoms and pharmaceuticals. The last two appear to suffer most from the cost of inefficiencies induced by regulatory obstacles. Automobiles is another industry for which non-Europe is a major cost factor.

Inter-company link-ups and corporate expansion are an expensive business, of course, even in a home market. Costs are front-loaded and benefits are, by and large, for the longer-term. But to the deadweight costs inherent in any business cooperation are added, at the European level, a regulatory diversity so complex that, with limited exceptions, only larger companies can manage the more integrated forms of cross-frontier links. Thus transborder operations involving smaller companies are normally limited to marketing. Otherwise smaller business is in the main excluded from the European game. Costs make many of the more ambitious forms of cooperation almost the *chasse gardée* of big businesses. And even they pay for it. Among others, in the five following ways:

1 Accounting costs and 'fiscal suspicion'
The extra administrative burden imposed by different auditing and fiscal systems was estimated by the report at between 10%-30% of the costs of the company departments involved.

High on the list of problems faced by integrated European multinationals are differing accounting standards. These lead to the considerable administrative costs of standardizing the accounts (or 'translating' them) for the purposes of central management control. Indeed, most large companies have to produce three sets of figures: those conforming to the national requirements of the parent company (including the consolidated or 'translated' accounts of subsidiaries); national accounts for each subsidiary; and a standardized system specific to the company used by all of its units for the purposes of internal control. Add to this the different reporting dates and periods in different EC countries, and the effort required to avoid total confusion, let alone manage the company, can easily be imagined.

For all that, the tax problem is much more serious. Europe-wide companies are forced systematically to make costly adjustments to allay what is termed the 'fiscal suspicion' of competing national tax authorities. Such suspicion tends to view the daily exchange of goods, assets and know-how between affiliated companies located in different countries almost exclusively as an opportunity for tax evasion. This assumption on the part of the national tax collector, whether or not justified, in turn generates considerable administrative costs for companies – to say nothing of the limits that it imposes on company flexibility. That's to say, the freedom of the company to act as a single operation and not simply an aggregation of nationally distinct units.

These 'beggar-thy-neighbour' attempts made by national tax authorities to maximise their share of a European company's tax liability have grave consequences. In addition to their extravagant demands on corporate administration, they influence other key company decisions, including those on locating group management, production and R&D.

For example, the suspicion that transfer prices are being used to export profits from one tax jurisdiction to another makes it often difficult, according to the companies interviewed, for central R&D expenditure to be actually charged to subsidiaries. Indeed, they claimed that it was in fact easier for an independent firm to export items like software at its fair value than for affiliated companies to do so between themselves. There are more general problems too. Many companies cited the impossibility of reducing tax liability by off-setting losses in one branch with profits in another as very costly to their operations.

Transfer pricing policies practised in EC countries are, moreover, inconsistent – so inconsistent that, according to one respondent, a company *had* to be in an illegal situation somewhere. In fact 'Europe would grind to a halt if national legislation were fully applied'.

2 Discriminatory impact of national industrial policies

The discretionary application of national policy and regulations in areas like procurement, investment and R&D is a further cost billed to transborder operations.

The picture is varied, depending on the country. A country like Italy, for example, which is seeking to build up from scratch a national strategic potential in the telecom sector, may practise outright discrimination against foreign-owned subsidiaries. National R&D programmes, as in the case of consumer electronics in Germany, may be discontinued altogether if a whole sector passes into foreign hands. Authorities in countries with inward investment controls, like Spain, may link the take-over of attractive companies by foreign capital to the buying out of a national lame duck.

Local content is a common performance requirement for foreign investors seeking national procurement awards. Extreme examples of this are provided by the pharmaceutical sector. Companies surveyed in the research, for instance, claim that in Belgium the authorities 'rewarded' local production with higher prices. In Britain, it was suggested (by non-British companies), price controls are related to total investment, including R&D. This led European companies to 'overinvest' in British R&D activities: with 4% of the world pharmaceuticals market, the United Kingdom accounted for 10% of world research.

3 Product specifications

Divergent national product standards, in addition to their more general costs on the European economy (see Chapter 4), also have a specific impact on integrated business planning in Europe. A number of firms devote an excessive share of their R&D budgets to the adjustment of their technology to different national settings.

Apart from anything else, this practice obviously reduces the economies of scale for R&D which would otherwise accrue to integrated European companies in a truly integrated European market. Obstacles of this sort are particularly harsh in sectors like telecommunications and mass-produced electronic components.

As a general rule, the problems encountered here mean substantial extra costs to European multinationals and often discourage them from increasing the level of internal integration. Paradoxically, for smaller business, the problems caused by differing product standards push them in a different direction and encourage them to seek production partners in other EC countries to adapt their product to local standards, get type-approval etc.

4 Trade obstacles

Border delays and uncertainties are causing increasing problems to the trade in components between the different entities of European transnational companies. Indeed the transborder activity of such firms, with their tight logistics planning, is hampered by border controls even more than arms-length trade (for latter see Chapter 2). A further problem is the intra-EC applications of strategic export controls drawn up by COCOM (the Coordinating Committee of NATO countries plus Japan controlling strategic exports). The COCOM controls mean hold-ups at the border, difficulties in carrying out speedy repairs (because spare-parts may be on the COCOM lists), not to speak of differences between national COCOM lists which cause uneven application and further problems at intra-EC frontiers. The problem of export controls was mentioned repeatedly by firms in the electronics and advanced engineering sectors, maybe indicating an area of future EC action in foreign trade policy.

5 Employment regulation

The social costs involved in the transfer of managerial and technical personnel between affiliated companies is a further problem for transborder business in the EC. The degree of 'portability' of social security benefits, notably pension schemes, is limited because they are tailored to national tax systems and/or related to public insurance schemes. In practice the firm must pay twice, raising salary costs for expatriates by 10%–15%.

Differing impact on different sectors

The aggregate costs borne by transborder business link-ups, as a result of inefficiencies caused by these regulatory burdens, are not spread evenly between sectors. Sectors combining high levels of both technology and regulation emerge as worst off. Mature industries like automobiles and consumer electronics fare somewhat better but their integrated European structures are nonetheless severely penalised. Industries where performance can be optimized at lower levels of transborder integration come off best. (The cost of the sector-specific barriers affecting industries considered here are in most cases outlined in detail in Chapter 7, but Chapter 7 takes no account of non-specific regulatory burdens like divergent accounting, company law and tax requirements.)

Pharmaceuticals and telecommunications
These are strongly regulated and protected industries with a high incidence of almost all of the obstacles cited above. Particularly costly are the problems associated in overcoming barriers posed by national industrial policies and technical standards.

Automobiles
The problems cited by this group include national industrial protection, shortfalls in economies of scale due to differences in technical standards, and substantial administrative costs for highly integrated operations. Total costs linked to transborder activity were estimated at higher than both average profit margins and average R&D expenditure of firms in these sectors.

Textiles and machine tools
Companies in these two groups were characterized by high specialization, with fairly decentralized manufacturing units each producing independent parts of the product range. Subsidiaries were typically involved in marketing or service functions. There were few problems with technical standards. Transborder costs for companies in these sectors were much lower than for telecoms, pharmaceuticals and automobiles.

Serious as this overall situation appears, it is not the full picture. There would be further savings which would occur if regulatory obstacles were eliminated or significantly reduced. For in a real European home market, the pattern of business competition and thus of business structures may be expected to change substantially. True, transborder business links may in some cases be reduced if, for example, national performance requirements (like local content) imposed on certain industrial sectors lessen. But the positive impact of the removal of obstacles would be much greater. The prospect is that it would unleash a growth of trans-European business link-ups which are being foregone by companies not big enough to bear the costs.

It is clear that it is for this latter category of companies, currently excluded from playing the transborder business game, that the potential is the most exciting. Under true home market conditions, they may be expected to become involved in the new forms of transborder organization, like cooperative networking, with which industry is now experimenting. Cooperative networking, which can exist with minority equity participation or indeed even in its absence, provides a form of business link-up which meets companies' needs for both strategic control and flexibility. The latter in particular is of increasing importance, since it allows firms to provide the efficient short-term market responsiveness which is becoming the essence of modern business organization.

6   The costs for the service sectors

The service sectors play a role of growing importance in the European economy. But their potential for much more significant growth is being artificially pinned back by regulations and practices which significantly inhibit the free flow of services and thus the free play of competition between companies supplying them. Moreover, because of the role they play in servicing business as a whole, the stunted growth they suffer is passed on into the economy at large.

Government regulations, while aiming primarily at prudential or safety objectives, often constitute a barrier to market entry to many of the sectors considered below. This is the case, for instance, for many activities in financial services (banking, insurance and securities), while the role of technical regulations, standards and procurement impact heavily on the Community market, or the absence of it, for telecommunications services. The regulatory situation is more varied for other business services – eg. advertising, engineering, computing and legal services.

Financial Services

Overview
Substantial economic gains may be expected from real integration of European financial services markets. This is because of the unique, pivotal role played by financial services in catalysing the economy as a whole. Removal of barriers here, and of the costs linked to them, would lead to three interlocking effects : a surge in the competitivity of the sector itself; a knock-on boost to all business using its increasingly efficient services; and, more generally, a new and positive influence on the conduct of macro-economic policy in the EC.[13]

An order of magnitude of Ecu 22 billion, based on calculations and assumptions detailed in the report, is the estimate for the gains forecast by the research for the eight EC countries studied as a result of integration of the three main areas of financial service activity: banking and credit, insurance, brokerage and securities. Core element of this calculation was the analysis of the present price differentials between the eight markets – France, Germany, Italy, Spain, the UK and the Benelux countries – for a representative

Table 6.1 Percentage differences in prices of standard financial products compared with the average of the four lowest national prices*

Name of standard service	Description of standard service	Belgium	Germany	Spain	France	Italy	Luxembourg	Netherlands	UK
Banking services									
1. Consumer credit	Annual cost of consumer loan of 500 ECU. Excess interest rate over money market rates	-41	136	39	n.a.	121	-26	31	121
2. Credit cards	Annual cost assuming 500 ECU debit. Excess interest rate over. money market rates	79	60	26	-30	89	-12	43	16
3. Mortgages	Annual cost of home loan of 25,000 ECU. Excess interest rate over money market rates	31	57	118	78	-4	n.a.	-6	-20
4. Letters of credit	Cost of letter of credit of 50,000 ECU for three months	22	-10	59	-7	9	27	17	8
5. Foreign exchange drafts	Cost to a large commercial client of purchasing a commercial draft for 30,000 ECU.	6	31	196	56	23	33	-46	16
6. Travellers cheques	Cost for a private consumer of purchasing 100 ECU worth of travellers cheques	35	-7	30	39	22	-7	33	-7
7. Commercial loans	Annual cost (including commissions and charges) to a medium sized firm of a commercial loan of 250,000 ECU	-5	6	19	-7	9	6	43	46

Insurance services

1. Life insurance	Average annual cost of term (life) insurance	78	5	37	33	83	66	-9	-30
2. Home insurance	Annual cost of fire and theft cover for house valued at 70,000 ECU with 28,000 ECU contents	-16	3	-4	39	81	57	17	90
3. Motor insurance	Annual cost of comprehensive insurance, 1.6 litre car, driver 10 years experience, no claims bonus	30	15	100	9	148	77	-7	-17
4. Commercial fire and theft	Annual cover for premises valued at 387,240 ECU & stock at 232,344 ECU	-9	43	24	153	245	-15	-1	27
5. Public liability cover	Annual premium for engineering company with 20 employees and annual turnover of 1.29 million ECU	13	47	60	117	77	9	-16	-7

Brokerage services

1. Private equity transactions	Commission costs of cash bargain of 1440 ECU	36	7	65	-13	-3	7	114	123
2. Private gilts transaction	Commission costs of cash bargain of 14000 ECU	14	90	217	21	-63	27	161	36
3. Institutional equity transactions	Commission cots of cash bargain of 288000 ECU	26	69	153	-5	47	68	26	-47
4. Institutional gilt transactions	Commission costs of cash bargain of 7.2 million ECU	284	-4	60	57	92	-36	21	n.a.

* The figures show the extent to which financial product prices, in each country, are above a low reference level. Each of these price differences implies a theoretical potential price fall from existing price levels to the low reference level (see also Table 6.2, p.42).

basket of financial services (consumer credit, mortgage, etc), and of their price development under the competitive pressures of integration.

Examples of existing price differences abound (see Table 6.1), reflecting differing competitive conditions in EC member states. Divergences are frequently of the order of 50% or more. Notably wide margins are found in prices charged for motor insurance, home loans, consumer credit and securities.

A few figures illustrate the present size of the Community's financial services sector, and its pervasive influence over the economy as a whole. Value-added by the credit and insurance sectors alone accounted for some 6.5% of the EC's gross domestic product in 1985. This was generated by 3% of the EC workforce whose share in overall compensation, however, was 6%, indicating earnings of around twice the Community average. In the eight countries studied, insurance premiums were estimated at around 5% of Gdp, while bank loans and stock market capitalization were respectively 142% and 116% of Gdp.

Substantial barriers beginning to be eroded by EC action
A variety of barriers, legislative and other, continue to hinder integration in banking, insurance and securities. High on the list of these obstacles is one with a multi-sectoral impact on financial services: controls on capital movements.

Despite progress toward the removal of this constraint, strict controls are still applied in four EC countries (Spain, Greece, Portugal and Ireland), and France and Italy are only now in the process of liberalizing them. Exchange controls have been removed in the UK and Denmark, and Germany and the Benelux countries allow free capital movement subject, however, to reporting and authorization procedures on certain transactions. The Commission has proposed a two-phase plan for fully integrating EC capital markets by 1992, and the first of these phases, which took effect February 1987, liberalizes cross-border transactions in unlisted securities, unit trusts, national securities on foreign stock markets and longer-term trade credits.

Banks Beyond exchange controls lies a variety of other obstacles affecting financial services. Thus in the banking sector, although freedom of establishment has been achieved through EC legislation and little overt discrimination remains, it appears difficult for many banks to compete successfully in other Community countries because new establishment involves considerable costs not borne by existing domestic banking networks. These difficulties are aggravated in certain countries (eg. Spain, Italy) by restrictions on foreign

40

acquisitions or participations in local banks. Moreover, even after removal of exchange controls, selling banking services across internal EC borders would be hampered in certain Community countries by some residual banking regulations (eg. preventing cross-border soliciting of deposits, and rules in some member states against bank involvement in the securities' business). An EC proposal (for a 'second Council directive on credit institutions'), made in January 1988 and targetted for adoption by 1989, should ensure that such legislative barriers are swept away by 1992.

Insurance As in the banking sector, there is freedom to establish (despite major residual differences in national regulations), but restrictions on doing direct cross-frontier business remain significant. Indeed, most member states (eg. Germany) simply do not permit non-national insurers to solicit directly without a local permanent establishment and this, coupled with discriminatory tax measures, continues to insulate many national insurers from outside competition. However, a significant step towards increased competition, particularly for larger commercial risk cover, was taken in February 1988 when the EC Council reached agreement on a proposed directive whose formal adoption is expected before year-end.

Stock market and securities Apart from residual exchange controls (clearly a significant barrier in this sector), integration is trammelled by a variety of national regulations. These include rules preventing foreigners being licensed as brokers, imposition in some countries of discriminatory taxes on purchases of foreign securities, and re-strictions on balance sheet holdings of foreign securities. Once again a number of EC directives have been adopted in this area, and others – eg. the directive, effective as of 1989, enabling unit trusts to market Community-wide – should continue the impetus to liberalization.

Gains from removal of barriers
The Ecu 22 billion gain from completing the EC internal market was calculated on the basis of estimates of the prices of a standard set of financial products before and after the removal of regulatory barriers, including abolition of exchange controls.

Table 6.1 (see above) lists the services investigated and the price differences prevailing for them between the eight countries studied. For each of these products, current prices were estimated which, when coverted into Ecus, enable intra-country comparisons.

Using this comparative analysis as a starting point, the research analysed the *potential* price falls and, within this overall potential, the *expected* price falls subsequent to the removal of regulatory barriers. The outcome of this calculation is given in Table 6.2 over.

Table 6.2   Potential and expected price falls for financial services

	Potential price falls (%)	Range of expected price falls	Mid points of the expected range of price falls (%)*
1. Spain	34	16 – 26	21
2. Italy	28	9 – 19	14
3. France	24	7 – 17	12
4. Belgium	23	6 – 16	11
5. Germany	25	5 – 15	10
6. Luxemburg	17	3 – 13	8
7. UK	13	2 – 12	7
8. Netherlands	9	0 – 9	4

* Ranges of 10 percentage points wide have been assumed, with the above expected price falls as the mid points.

This shows the greatest expected fall in Spain, somewhat smaller falls in Italy, France, Belgium and Germany, and the most modest reductions in the United Kingdom, Luxembourg, and the Netherlands. The difference between potential and expected price falls reflects the fact that, even after removing regulatory obstacles, differences in financial markets would subsist due to unavoidable variations in risk, custom and other local conditions.

Broken down between the eight countries studied, the share per country in this expected gain for financial service consumers is given below in Table 6.3. The largest overall benefits are registered by the United Kingdom and Germany where price falls, though relatively modest, are leveraged upwards by the size of their financial services markets.

Table 6.3   Estimated gain in consumer surplus resulting from integration of European credit and insurance markets

	ECUs billion
Belgium	0.7
Germany	4.6
Spain	3.2
France	3.7
Italy	4.0
Luxemburg	0.1
Netherlands	0.3
United Kingdom	5.1
Total	21.7

Telecommunications services

Overview

Rapid communication of information is an essential both for integrating Europe's markets and for the modernization and competitivity of the companies operating in it. Telecom services – starting with the phone but ranging through 'value-added services' like telex, fax and vision (now able to be carried together on an integrated network) – are the vehicle for meeting these needs. The importance of providing the telecom sector with a regulatory framework suited to meeting these demands was recognized in 1987 by the EC Commission's 'Green Paper on the Development of the Common Market for Telecommunications Services and Equipment'.

With the arrival of new digital signalling and switching systems, telecoms are increasingly converging with the digital technology of the data-processing sector, a convergence epitomized by ISDN ('integrated services digital network'). As a result digital telecoms do for computers what the motorway network did for the automobile. They provide the so-called 'global information highway' – not just for the computer industry but for all sectors relying on accurate data and its speedy transmission to stay competitive.

The trouble with the EC's emerging information highway is its many national road blocks – and even the problems of the incompatible equipment being used in the construction of its various sections. Illustrated below, these barriers take a variety of forms – including divergent norms, generally high tariffs for network users, and the overweening presence of monopoly service suppliers (the Community's PTTs) essentially dictating in their different national enclaves the rules according to which the highway is accessed and used.

Community's PTT revenue from the telecom service sector totalled some Ecu 61 billion in 1985 (see Table 6.4), or around four times the EC telecom equipment market (see Chapter 7). By comparison, the US market for services is twice the size of the EC sector. In the Community, voice telephony accounts for 85% – 90% of total PTT telecom revenues, with up to 10% deriving from fax and up to 5% from telex.

Barriers

The various obstacles hampering market integration and economic performance – differing standards, the monopoly powers of the PTTs etc. – impact on business in all sectors, not to speak of the private individual.

Table 6.4   National income from telecoms service provision (1985)

Country	Operating Income in mill. ECU
Belgium	1,406
Denmark	1,076
France	13,428
Germany	15,124
Greece	721
Italy	8,351
Ireland	624
Luxemburg	82
Netherlands	2,539
Portugal (CCT and CLT)	679
Spain	3,154
UK (BT only)	14,245
Total	61,429

Source: Telefonica/ITU (Exchange rates as of 1985)

Monopoly powers have fathered artificial price levels. Thus the tariffs set for long-distance international calls by PTTs are disproportionately greater than those for national long-distance connections. This is a fairly direct method of penalizing cross-frontier communication, be it for commercial or personal purposes.

Tariffs vary, sometimes significantly, between different EC countries. For certain sectors of business, this can lead to distortions in decisions on company location. The attraction of low telephone tariffs may, for example, determine where the host computers of data banks are located. Provision of telebanking services may, in turn, tend to be concentrated in financial markets with access to cost-effective telecom services.

Widespread limitations exist on the use of leased lines. Thus firms leasing lines from the PTT may be restricted in the use they can make of them as a vehicle for carrying cross-border telecom services for their clients. This acts as a double brake: first on business activity, and second, on the development of the value-added telecom services increasingly required for effective business performance.

Market fragmentation for services partly results from the knock-on effect of similar segmentation suffered by the telecom equipment sector (see Chapter 7). Exercise of monopoly powers, notably over national standards and procurement, has tended to result in overpriced and incompatible equipment, meaning in some cases that services are simply not available in certain national markets. Market entry barriers like this are on occasion justified on the grounds that foreign equipment might harm the local system.

Symptomatic of these obstacles are differences in videotex systems. The UK, France and Germany have developed their systems without coordination, and only now are attempts being made to rectify the situation. The problem facing Iveco, a FIAT affiliate, is a case in point. In France, a client can use the local videotex to select the model he wants, but German and Italian clients cannot yet plug in.

Market entry barriers can be more forthright. The national monopolies can simply prevent private companies from providing client-specific services. Private value-added networks for data transmission are not allowed to compete with the national monopoly in many EC countries. A new company planning to offer such services in France – to be formed by IBM and some French companies – would have been in violation of French law.[14]

To tackle these and other obstacles, the EC's Green Paper on telecoms has adopted a selective approach to the problem of national regulation and the barriers that can arise as a result. It suggests that for basic telecom networks, especially voice telephony, national administrations should maintain their traditional role. However, the Green Paper draws a line between 'reserved services' of this sort and 'competitive services', ie. the value-added services (VAS) for which open competition is recommended. Measures to enhance inter-operability are also proposed, as is a European Telecommunications Standards Institute.

Costs

Companies and individuals have to bear heavy burdens resulting from market and trade barriers. These are costed in Table 6.5, whose two right-hand columns provide estimates of gains following removal of these costs, for respectively two different levels of liberalization.

The first of these, taking as its point of departure implementation of the minimum liberalization requirements spelt out in the Green Paper, indicates that these gains could amount to around Ecu 2 billion. The important components of this overall figure are the benefits, including economies of scale, resulting for the service network as a result of lower equipment costs leading to lower tariffs; and those stemming from greater competition for non-reserved services.

Full network competition, the subject of the right-hand column, would mean additional gains. The principal quantifiable benefit in

45

Measures	Minimum Green Paper Effect	'Full Network Competition' Effect[1]
1) Lower equipment costs (see Chapter 7) lead to lower tariffs and thereby economies of scale and fill in the network use	0.75 billion ECU per annum savings[2]	slightly larger
2) More competitive 'Non-Reserved Services'		
a) easier CPE certification, increased product variety, lower CPE prices, larger network use	0.5–0.7 billion ECU savings	not estimated
b) liberalize VAS	0.3–0.4 billion ECU savings by 1990	larger, because few network restrictions
c) open network provision	0.2 billion ECU savings by 1990	not estimated
3) Tariff Reforms (closer to cost)	not estimated	4 billion ECU p.a.

1 for long-distance and international traffic
2 these gains exclude the direct savings on equipment purchases.

this scenario would be an Ecu 4 billion annual benefit from a lowering of tariffs for long-distance and international traffic.

Other business services

Outline
First impressions, gained from users of business services, are that there are no great barriers to cross-frontier activity in areas like advertising, public relations, engineering and legal services. But these impressions, reflecting a generally low level of awareness of obstacles among service users, are misleading. This is one of the chief conclusions emerging from research into the costs borne by business services as a result of European market fragmentation, and into the economic benefits which may be expected to accrue from their removal. The research, including a survey of users and providers of such services in France, Germany, Italy, the United Kingdom and the Benelux countries, comes up with an assessment of the overall EC turnover of the sector in 1986 broken down by sub-sector (see Table 6.6).

Table 6.6   Business services turnover, 1986 (total EC)*

Sector	Turnover (bn Ecu)
Engineering & Related Services	7.5
Consultancy	3.5
Advertising**	57
Public Relations	2
Computing Services	13
Research & Development	15
Financial Review (accounting, audit)	13
Legal Services	13
Total	124.0

* Excluding operational services (eg. catering)
** Including media costs

Taken as a whole, business services make an important contribution to the Community economy, with their value added accounting for around 4% of the EC's gross domestic product.

Barriers and their impact
Understandably, perhaps, suppliers of business services are much more aware than their customers of the hurdles to be crossed in delivering cross-frontier client service. These include, with varying impact depending on the sector: tax and financial barriers, restrictions on carrying out business abroad, differing product regulations and illiberal public procurement. The types of barriers affecting the various sectors, together with an indication of their overall significance, are evaluated (see Table 6.7).

Illustrative of the problems created by these barriers is the complaint from a UK computer services company about differences in standards. More generally, in sectors like advertising and public relations, there are sharp differences between EC countries in the conditions for doing business, often with important knock-on effects on competition. Thus in Germany, advertising and PR firms are barred from raising money through public share issues, leaving them vulnerable to competition from UK companies with unrestricted access to stock markets. Using this facility, Saatchi & Saatchi is now not only Europe's no. 1, but the world's leading advertising/PR group. Still in the advertising sector, an obstacle the survey shows as significant is constituted by conflicting regulations on TV advertising

Table 6.7   Barriers to trade in business services

Sector	Nature of barriers	Overall significance of barrier
Engineering and related	Government procurement Technical standards Licensing of professionals Tax treatment	i) Engineers: barriers quite significant ii) Architect: barriers very restrictive
Computing services	Government and PTI procurement of computer services	UK reports this barrier
Research and development	Bias in government procurement	Reported by Germany (demand side interview)
Commercial communications	Satellite broadcasting barriers	
	Differences in advertising law (regarding permissible advertising material)	
	Limitations on media time for advertising	Generally regarded as reasonably free market
	Lack of access to equity markets (Germany)	
	Qualifications of professionals	
Legal services	Freedom to practice	Not generally recognized by professional bodies as significant
Operational services	None	Largely unregulated market
Management consultancy	None	No barriers of significance

whose impact is increasing. To resolve these problems the Commission has proposed a measure harmonizing national rules on advertising on public TV programmes.

Four main benefits resulting from removal of barrier-related costs
These barriers lead to costs both for providers and users of services whose removal, according to the research, could over time lead to global savings of up to Ecu 9.2 billion.

First, they increase the costs for companies seeking to market their services abroad, they hinder expansion and reduce the quality and range of services available. Service suppliers expect that increased competition resultant on completion of the internal market will lead to consumers gaining in quality perhaps even more than in lower prices. Competitors are not likely to enter new markets on a price-cutting basis but rather by offering improved products. Nevertheless, costs to service companies could be reduced by up to Ecu 3.5 billion.

Second, a knock-on effect of this is the costs for all sectors currently using business services – taking the form of lower output than would be the case in an integrated market. Improved business services should lead to increases in the competitivity of the companies buying in these services in relation to their rivals outside the Community, in addition to creating more even competitive conditions within the EC. This factor is expected to boost sales of service user companies by up to an estimated Ecu 3 billion.

Third, over and above cost savings for business service suppliers noted above, there should be further gains for them as their output rises in response to the extra demand created by the completion of the internal market in all sectors. Increased demand for services from this source is estimated in a spread of Ecu 0.7–2.5 billion. Also linked to the impulse given to demand by general market integration is another gain distinguished by the research under the name 'externalization'. This is that companies actually or potentially using business services will tend increasingly to buy in services from outside, rather than attempt to provide them themselves from within. Under the pressure of intensified competition, user companies will be forced to concentrate on those areas of their activities that they are best at. For these companies, cost savings in externalizing services might be of the order of Ecu 100–200m. Externalization will also have a favourable employment effect in the service-providing companies.

7 Costs in the manufacturing sector

How does the array of barriers signalled in the preceding pages impact on individual industrial activities in the EC? What, from this more specific perspective, are the costs they impose – be they the costs directly linked to barriers, or those which reflect more general benefits foregone because of the existence of barriers?

A widespread finding of the six short industry case studies outlined below is that, as in the service sectors (Chapter 6), the size of the longer-term gains to be had from EC market integration is much greater than the costs directly saved by removing barriers.

The sectors examined below (telecoms, motor manufacturing, foodstuffs, building products, textiles and clothing, and pharmaceuticals) together represent 43% of the Community's industrial output and provide 13% of the economy's total value added. They were selected to give as broad a picture as possible of the range of problems manufacturing companies can face as a result of market barriers. Understandably, the picture shows that barriers vary in impact depending on the basic characteristics of the sector concerned.

Nonetheless, one general point emerges clearly. This is the pervasive impact of standards and technical regulations in most of the industries considered. By contrast, the procurement barrier tends to pose particular problems in areas like telecommunications and pharmaceuticals, but is relatively minor for some of the other branches considered below.

Telecommunications equipment

Overview

The costs imposed on the EC telecommunications equipment industry by national regulation and practice are substantial, as is their ripple effect throughout the economy. They are getting greater as business everywhere, under the twin pressures of rapid technological changes and the size of the market share required to amortize their development, is being forced to go global.

In varying degrees, these factors apply to the three main sub-sectors of the Community's telecom equipment industry, namely :

- *customer premises equipment* (CPE) – terminal equipment like telephones, telefax and telex machines (CPE took a 24% share of the EC's telecom equipment market in 1986);
- *transmission equipment* – wires, cables, antennas etc. needed to transmit voice, data and vision (13% of EC market);
- *central office equipment* (CO) – switching equipment needed to connect the various transmission paths (with 47% of the market, CO is easily the largest segment).

Overall costs are estimated by the research to be as much as some 25% of the $17.5 billion estimated value of the total telecom equipment Community market in 1986. The main item in this bill is restrictive procurement practices, followed by divergences in national standards and restrictive certification policies.

Measures, set out in the EC Commission's 1985 Internal Market White Paper and its 1987 Green Paper on Telecommunications (see diagram below), seek to limit the costs imposed by national behaviour in these areas. Even though total removal of costs – implying a fully competitive market – may be an ambitious expectation, considerable benefits are in prospect including, according to the report, significant gains from economies of scale.

EC Telecom Green Paper*

Among the actions it envisages:

- phased 40% liberalization of public procurement, post-1992 a directive for 100% opening;
- creation of a European Standards Institute to accelerate standards and technical specifications, and ease certification;
- clear separation of regulatory and market functions of telecom authorities.

* 'Green Paper on the Development of the Common Market for Telecommunications Services and Equipment'.

Improvements in EC industry and market organization are needed urgently. In 1986, the Community represented about 19% of the world market as against 38% for the US and 9% for Japan. Moreover, the EC market is forecast to grow up to 1990 at around half the rate for the US (6.6%) and Japan (5%). Even the larger EC member states have small markets – compared to Japan, let alone the US – and these are segmented, there being little intra-EC trade. Not surprisingly, European industry's competitivity is declining. The EC

51

sector's surplus, which shrank from Ecu 1.5 billion in 1984 to Ecu 1.2 billion in 1986, is mainly obtained from trade with smaller countries; by contrast it ran a deficit with the US and Japan of respectively Ecu 620m and 685m in 1986.

Barriers reinforced by market power of regulatory authorities
Differing standards, restrictive certification and protectionist public purchasing are the main barriers which segment the Community market into national entities and sustain the symbiotic relationship, within most member states, between the industry and the national PTTs (posts, telephone and telecommunications authorities). Despite signs of incipient liberalization (eg. the privatization of British Telecom), this relationship remains the key fact of life in the EC telecom equipment business.

National telecom authorities have a crucial dual role. They set the rules of the game and, as regards purchasing for most equipment, are its major players. Easily the greatest buyers of telecom equipment – achieving shares of 80% in some countries – these bodies often use their purchasing muscle to support national producers and sometimes deliberately to exclude external competitors. One result of this is artificially high prices. At the beginning of the decade, equipment in Europe was 80%-100% more expensive than in the US. Moreover, there are important price differences within the Community (see Table 7.1)

Equally impressive, in its own way, is the performance of the national authorities as industry regulators. The barriers to market entry they create by protectionist national procurement have

Table 7.1   High EC prices for telecom equipment – Overpricing in EC markets compared with competitive world levels[15]

Country	Central Office	% price deviation Transmission	Consumer Premises
Belgium	120	60	40
Denmark	30	30	40
France	50	30	40
Germany	100	50	80
Greece	n.a.	n.a.	n.a.
Italy	100	30	40
Ireland	n.a.	n.a.	n.a.
Luxemburg	n.a.	n.a.	n.a.
Netherlands	50	n.a.	60
Portugal	n.a.	n.a.	n.a.
Spain	50	40	30
United Kingdom	40	30	40

traditionally been supplemented by their further control over product standardization and certification. This has led to incompatible standards and 'input specificity' – meaning that new equipment must be compatible with existing installations, thus discouraging new entrants to the market.

Barriers also impact on equipment sold directly to private customers. A driver wishing to use a car telephone on a trip from Germany via Belgium to the UK has to install three different systems. A telefax machine installed in France has to fulfil somewhat different certification requirements from those required, for example, in Denmark or Greece. For private automatic branch exchanges (PABX), the divergences in costs and procedures are evident from the following table.

Table 7.2   Type approval procedures: fees and delays

Country	Fee charged	Average delay
Belgium	12,500–56,000 BF	3–6 months
France	n.a.	1 year
Germany	varies according to testing costs incurred	6 months–1 year
Italy	varies according to testing costs incurred	6 months–1 year
United Kingdom	£10 000 modems up to £100 000 PABXs	If no modification necessary: 3 months
United States	No charge	Less than 10 weeks

Source: Deutsches Institut für Wirtschaftsforschung, Study prepared for the Commission of the EC, 1986

Costs and economies of scale
The costs inherent in the market fragmentation caused by these barriers are estimated by the research in a range of around Ecu 3–4.8 billion. The calculation is made on the basis of the difference between, on the one hand, the performance expected from industry in the competitive environment sought by EC proposals and, on the other, the forward projection of the present situation unaided by Community action.

Table 7.3 examines the gains to be achieved from the removal of the two basic cost areas – standards and procurement. These gains reflect both static gains (ie. those brought about by the downward matching of prices directly following the removal of barriers), and dynamic gains (those achieved over the longer run, eg. sales growth, economies of scale, etc. resulting on market integration). In the case of public procurement, the effects of two alternative degrees of liberalization have been calculated: 40% and 100% (see also diagram on Telecom Green Paper p.51).

In general, economies of scale are imperative if European industry is to absorb the costs of developing the new generation of digital switching equipment. Losses from unrealized economies of scale are greatest for central office equipment (CO) where software costs are currently estimated at above 50% of value added.

Despite the manufacturing scale required by digitalization, the EC market is segmented into relatively small national entities in which typically several firms, often indigenous, are competing to supply only one national buyer. According to the report, savings of Ecu 1.25–1.5 billion would be gained by companies in the public switching sector as a result of rationalized standards and partially liberalized (40%) procurement. Assuming total procurement liberalization, a further gain of Ecu 1.3 billion would be realized.

The estimate is that the potential gains from economies of scale for the other market segments, including CPE and transmission equipment, are not as high as for CO. However, they are significant and, as digitalization begins to make possible network integration (ISDN – integrated services digital networks), they are increasing.

Table 7.3   Telecom equipment: gains from EC market integration (static and dynamic combined) – Ecu billions

	Effects of standardization	Effects of procurement liberalization	
		40%	100%
Product:			
Central Office Switching	0.45–0.7	0.8	1.3
Transmission	0.2	0.4	0.5
Terminal Equipment (CPE)	0.1	0.4	1.0
Other	0.1	0.4	0.9
Total	0.85–1.1	2.0 + 0.2*	3.7

* dynamic effect spread throughout all sectors.

Automobiles

Overview

Contributing almost 6% of value-added in EC manufacturing and employing 7% of its workforce, the automobile industry is by any standards a key sector of the European economy. In 1985, EC manufacturers accounted for about 40% of world passenger car output. Yet a range of barriers, including divergent technical regulations and massive tax differences, continue to fragment the Community market and impede the rational organization of a Europe-wide industry supplying it. Overall cost of the impediments signalled in the White Paper, or the savings which would over time result from their removal, in particular through economies of scale, is estimated at Ecu 2.6 billion, or 5% of the industry's unit costs.

These are the essential conclusions of the research report which was based, inter alia, on a detailed survey of auto manufacturers and suppliers. A particular focus of the report was how the post-1992 integrated market would impact on two key phases of industry activity – design and engineering, and manufacturing and assembly. Clearing away the regulatory diversity enabling industry to gear up these functions for the challenge of the 1990s is given additional incentive by the Community's market potential. By 1987, the EC had already overtaken the US to become the world's largest single car market.

A single market – but only in name

The trouble is that the world's largest single car market is single only in name. The range of obstacles hindering its effective integration, and likewise the matching rationalization of supply, provide a quintessential roll-call of Common Market disunity. This list, for reasons of space, is outlined here in abridged form:

fiscal barriers:

- taxation levels on car sales different in virtually all EC countries, ranging from 12% in Luxembourg to some 200% in Denmark and Greece;
- divergent policies on the refunding of VAT for company purchases of vehicles;
- distortion of competitive conditions by excessive aid to 'national champion' companies (grants, loans, equity injections, debt write-offs);
- use of fiscal incentives in some countries (Netherlands, Germany,

Luxembourg and Denmark) to encourage sales of vehicles built to differing emission and noise standards.

physical barriers:
- documentary and inspection requirements at intra-EC borders, with attendant delays resulting in loss of time and money in the shipping of components;
- differences in communications standards beween EC member states which impede cooperation in vehicle development and production.

technical barriers:
- lack of single EC-wide type approval procedure, requiring costly and time-consuming duplication of cars and tests;
- unique national vehicle equipment requirements, eg side repeater flasher lights in Italy, reclining driver's seat in West Germany, right-hand drive and dim-dip lighting in the UK, yellow headlamp bulbs in France, and unique rear reflectors in Germany.

Outlook for cost savings
Creating real European home market conditions by removing such regulatory barriers – a key example being the absence of full EC type approval (see also Chapter 4) – should accelerate current trends in industrial reorganization and technological change both in car and component manufacturing.

However, the challenge is not just the removal of obstacles but, in addition, the circumstances which allow these barriers to lead to such great price differences. In this respect the situation is particularly aggravated when divergent national standards are compounded by distribution arrangements which tend to segment the market.

Getting maximum gains from an integrated EC car market also depends on developments in other areas. Thus a fully-integrated telecoms sector (see above) and elimination of border red-tape (Chapter 2) would do much to facilitate the auto industry's component trade.

For 90 auto components surveyed, the research found that the European supply industry is providing many of the major components at rates far under 500,000 sets per annum. Sizeable economies of scale could be achieved if this level were reached. Sub-optimal production arises partly because carmakers are awarding the supply of a single part or assembly to several suppliers, and partly because of too many car models. A key economy of scale for European motor

56

manufacturing would be the reduction in the number of car-platforms needed. Platforms are vehicle floor-plan designs to which common components are attached in the areas of running gear, suspension, and steering, and which, through relatively little changes, can be used for different car models. Today 30 platforms are used in the EC for passenger volume cars produced by the six majors (VW, Volvo, Renault, Fiat, Ford and GM), but in the fully integrated market conditions sought for 1992 this could be reduced to 21 involving platform-sharing between several manufacturers.

Market integration, with gains of this sort, will result in savings in unit costs of around 5%, according to the research, or just over Ecu 2.6 billion for Community manufacturers taken together. This saving is forecast to be partly attributable to direct cost reductions as a result of abolishing EC barriers, but in particular to economies of scale resulting from platform reductions.

Looked at through another prism, the overall Ecu 2.6 billion figure can be expressed in terms of savings in respectively variable and fixed costs. Dominating the variable cost savings of almost Ecu 900m is an estimated gain of Ecu 826m in labour costs. This reflects a dramatic improvement in labour productivity, itself a result of the rationalized organization of output. Savings of Ecu 1.7 billion in fixed costs are broken down as follows:

Table 7.4   Savings in fixed costs in the automobile sector

Savings in fixed costs	Ecu million
• tooling	571.7
• engineering	700.7
• warranty provision	175.3
• administration/finance	213.3
• advertising	42.3

To these gains must be added the potential increase in sales resulting from price reductions. It has been estimated that the EC's demand for cars might increase by around half a million units simply as a result of the drop in prices linked to the removal of barriers sought by the White Paper.

Foodstuffs

Overview
The foodstuffs sector, the biggest contributor to jobs and value-added of all EC industries, appears well-placed to confront

international competition in the 1990s. But appearances may be misleading, for two reasons. The first is that the industry trend towards global consolidation is dominated, Unilever and Nestlé apart (respectively the world's number 1 and 2), by US companies who fill the other eight places in the world's top ten. The second is that the Community market for foodstuffs, whose 320m consumers should provide European companies with a ready-made platform for a global challenge, is segmented by a range of trade barriers which, despite holding action by the EC, seem to be on the increase.

The sharpening of the strategic threat is one of the main results of European market fragmentation. Expressed in money terms, costs to the industry resulting from non-tariff barriers are estimated by the research in a spread of Ecu 500-1000m annually, not counting the inevitable restrictions in consumer choice. Savings of this size, which would follow the elimination of trade obstacles, represent 2%-3% of the total value added of a sector which alone accounts for just over 4% of the Community's gross domestic product. They are estimated to equal up to a two-year gain in the industry's productivity.

More than 200 non-tariff barriers, classified by researchers into five types (see Table 7.5), were identified as applying to intra-EC trade on the 10 product sectors in the five largest EC countries. These products were: biscuits and cake; chocolate and confectionery; ice-cream; beer; mineral water; soft drinks; spirits; pasta; soup; baby food. They were chosen because of their importance to EC trade, their value, and the likelihood of their being subject to significant trade barriers.

Table 7.5   Non-tariff barriers in foodstuffs

	Identified	% of Total
• Specific import restrictions	64	29.4
• Packaging/labelling laws	68	31.2
• Specific ingredient restrictions	33	15.1
• Content/denomination regulations	39	17.9
• Fiscal discrimination	14	6.4
	218*	100%

* This is the aggregate number of barriers affecting the 10 items studied in the five countries concerned.

58

Trade barriers at work

Examples of some of these trade obstacles show the types of problems that a prospective exporter can run up against in selling to another EC country, to say nothing of the market distortions and the sub-optimal business structures which these barriers nurture. The report considers them among the main reasons responsible for the low growth in the industry's intra-EC trade since the late 1970s.

Soft drinks A non-nutritive sweetener, aspartame, is used for the 'diet' segment of the soft drink industries in North America and in most EC countries – but not all. Aspartame cannot be used in soft drinks in Spain (nor could it until early 1988 in France). One result of this specific ingredient restriction is that in France, for example, a mass diet segment does not exist. Without the barrier, it is estimated that such a market segment would emerge, ultimately capturing 10%-15% of the soft drinks market.

Beer This is a product which illustrates several types of barriers at work. Probably the best-known example of a content/ denomination regulation – a rule which prevents a product from using a generic name unless it conforms to certain content requirements – is the German beer purity law.

The purity law, censured by the European Court of Justice in 1987, is also a good example of an import restriction. The result of its application has been a highly-fragmented German beer industry (1200 brewers, or 75% of the total number in the EC) and a strongly protected market (with imports about only 1% of consumption).

Meanwhile, an example of a fiscal law which could discriminate against importers is the wort taxation method for beer. Five EC countries levy excise taxes on beer prior to fermentation, less a set wastage allowance. Excise taxes for imports into these countries is levied on the final product. If a domestic producer can routinely beat the pre-set wastage factor, it may derive a cost advantage compared to an importer.

Labelling laws Differing practice here is a hallmark of EC countries, partly reflecting misapplication of Community legislation. Spain, for example, insists on labelling including health registration numbers – a requirement inconsistent with EC rules.

Barriers such as these are not only extensive but, according to the report, they have two other worrying characteristics. They appear to be on the increase and are difficult to eliminate once in place. And they often demonstrate a high degree of inventiveness and on occasion an uncanny sense of commercial timing on the part of their national authors. For instance:

Recycling laws in Denmark In 1977, the Danish government enacted decree 136 which banned the imports of soft drinks in non-refillable containers. Three years later the European Commission ruled against it, saying it violated the Rome Treaty's provisions on free intra-EC trade (Article 30). The government promptly replaced it with decree 397, which banned the sale of soft drinks and beer in non-refillable bottles, imported or domestic. While on the surface this appeared non-discriminatory, the fact is that the transportation costs of two-way bottles makes them impractical over about 200km – a distance easily exceeded when exporting to Denmark. Denmark has both the highest level of beer consumption per capita in Europe after Germany and a negligible level of imports as a percentage of consumption.

Health registration in Spain Health registration for food products in Spain was implemented at about the time of its accession to the Community. The result is that trade with Spain became more difficult from elsewhere in the EC after its accession than before. As one EC exporter put it, 'our products were readily acceptable by the Spanish govenment up until the time Spain joined the EC. Now we have to go through the registration procedure'.

Direct and indirect costs
The costs ascribable to the fragmentation of the Community market reflect two types of effect: direct and indirect. Direct effects (eg. reduction in labelling, packaging and ingredient costs resulting directly from trade barriers) are likely to be significant, but not as great as indirect effects (eg. longer-run improvements in consumer choice, trade and industrial structure).

The bulk of the direct costs, which the report evaluates at Ecu 500-1000m, are attributable to just six types of barriers. This concentration of costs is further underscored by the fact that two closely linked barriers – restrictions on vegetable fat in chocolate and ice-cream – alone account for over 40% of the total.

Clearly the benefits directly stemming from the removal of these costs are sizeable, but even more important are the indirect benefits – essentially improved consumer choice and industrial efficiency. As in some other sectors (eg. building materials) the longer-term, dynamic effects possess the greatest potential for economic gains.

Example of benefits for consumers in a real Community home market include:

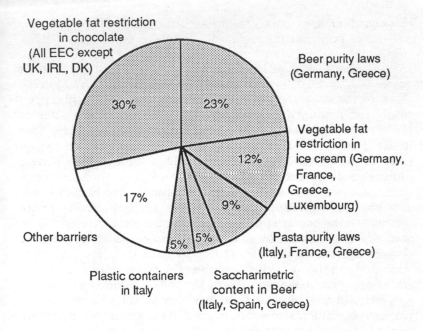

Chart 7.1   Distribution of total benefits in the foodstuffs sector (500–1000m Ecus)

- less expensive pasta products in Italy and France;
- a wider range of imported beers in Germany, and lighter beers in Italy and Spain;
- availability of diet soft drinks in France and Spain.

Dynamic gains in industrial efficiency should be heralded by the removal of intra-EC trade barriers. The European food industry, says the report, will likely undergo restructuring and consolidation. And none too soon, in view of the US-led global concentration of the industry which has occurred over the last decade.

The Americans are strongly placed to exploit the potential of the Community market. By contrast to the North American experience, EC companies operating in the common market do not in the majority of cases have an EC-wide strategy. Only about one in 10 firms do, together with a presence in the largest five Community countries. European food companies have by and large remained nationally focused. If they do not react to the pressures from trade deregulation by restructuring, EC-based food companies may get left behind.

Building products

Overview

At first glance, building products hardly seem to be a candidate for significant intra-Community trade. Many products – bricks, glass, lime, plaster etc. – are heavy, meaning that transport costs become a major factor; and indeed there are plenty whose price doubles every 150 km for this reason. Add to this customer requirements which differ widely from one country to another, apparently reflecting inherent divergences in national tastes, and the potential for large international exchange seems restricted.

Yet appearances are misleading. Surprisingly, the EC market for building products (worth Ecu 110 billion in 1985) already features extensive trans-border trade, according to the research report which analysed in particular the situation in France, Germany, Italy, the United Kingdom and Spain. It found that in these four countries, even for the heaviest products – cement, glass and other non-metallic minerals which make up 42% of the total market – exports and imports together accounted for more than half of consumption. Import penetration was significant in the markets of all of the four larger EC countries: 15% in Italy, 20% in Germany, 30% in France and 50% in the UK.

The potential for still greater cross-border business is currently pegged back by a range of barriers, above all myriad technical regulations and certification procedures differing from one EC country to another. Indeed so-called 'inherent' divergences in customer requirements may be largely a case of national tastes determined by national regulations. Costs directly associated with these and other barriers to trade in building materials are put at Ecu 820m for the Community. For the five largest member states the additional longer term gain expected from EC-wide deregulation – as industry improves its economies of scale – is estimated at some Ecu 1.7 billion.

The barriers: national regulations and the North/South divide

The picture emerging from the research is one of technical regulations unevenly spread throughout a Community which is split, in this respect, along a North South divide. Countries like Germany and France possess the most demanding requirements for prospective importers, while Italy and Spain, for example, have less demanding regulations. Southern countries often accept foreign technical standards and regulations. The UK presents something of a special case. Although British standards are significantly different from those used elsewhere in the EC, their use is not mandatory.

Product standards and certification procedures (the latter often lasting years rather than months) head an impressive list of trade barriers which also include procurement preferences, national requirements for contractors and building regulations.

A striking but not untypical example of the administrative costs and delays faced by transborder trade is the case of a French producer of girders which took about five years to obtain the technical certification needed to sell in Germany. More generally, the report shows that as many as 70% of the products it analysed face problems in complying with foreign technical regulations and, indeed, about 60% do not meet those regulations.

On the basis of the EC-wide survey of the industry conducted by the research, 85% of companies interviewed identified Germany and France as the markets where technical certification was most difficult to pass. In these countries the number of technical regulations is higher, and their influence on the choices of engineers, architects and buyers of building materials is greater. Exporters stressed that in Germany great attention is paid by construction firms, foremen and consumers to national regulations, with the result that it is almost impossible to sell products not meeting their requirements.

Some of the more discriminating technical standards and regulations relate to interior building materials like electrical appliances and sanitary ware. Constraints such as mains voltage, plug size and water pressure represent a serious impediment to their use Community-wide.

Cost savings
The direct effect of the removal of these trade barriers, which the White Paper is seeking through a programme for harmonising essential requirements (eg. stability, fire safety and health), will be a lowering of the costs borne by European exporters. Harmonization of technical regulations will reduce the heavy costs of obtaining certifications and, to a lesser extent, reductions will result from the removal of customs controls. A drop in transport costs (see Chapter 2) would also have a clear knock-on effect to the cost of transborder trade in building materials. Overall, direct savings for the EC industry should total around Ecu 820m.

Indirect savings, although only attained over a longer time-frame, are likely to be much more substantial. Estimated at Ecu 1.7 billion for the five larger EC countries, these will result from economies of scale forced on industry by the new competitive pressures – and opportunities – of an integrated European market. Research suggests that the more dynamic companies will strengthen their international strategies by increasing their size and rationalizing their marketing policies. Production shifts between EC countries will be less significant, because most companies will tend to set up subsidiaries in non-local markets. Firms will face two broad strategic choices – the 'Northern model' with very complicated regulatory requirements leading to use of sophisticated materials; or the less sophisticated 'Southern model'.

A further element to be factored into this general outlook is the particular problem architects face in operating across EC borders. This is highlighted in the Table dealing with barriers to trade in business services (see Table 6.7 p.48).

Textiles & clothing

Overview
The medicine of EC market integration has been administered to firms in the textile and clothing sector earlier than most. As a result, the industry presents something of a special case – it being perhaps the outstanding example of a manufacturing sector which has already reaped considerable benefits from progress towards home market conditions in Europe. In consequence, many cost savings and improvements in industry's economies of scale have already been achieved, and remaining trade barriers are of relatively small importance to Community producers. Nevertheless, further gains are achievable both for manufacturers' costs and for consumer prices.

The last two decades have been marked by major restructuring in the textiles and clothing sector in the Community and world-wide. There have been three main causes: a sustained surge in exports from the developing countries; a slowdown in consumption in the industrialized countries; and the increasing impact of European market integration. Restructuring has been favoured by EC trade measures the partial effect of which has been to keep Community prices above world levels. EC production of textiles and clothing, whose value added in 1985 was Ecu 54 billion, stopped rising in the mid-1970s. In the decade up to 1985 a million jobs were lost in the then ten EC member states, leaving sectoral employment at around 2.5 million, but still around 10% of the total for manufacturing.

As EC industrial restructuring has proceeded, companies have in many cases developed the flexibility needed to respond successfully to these pressures. In addition to marked advances in technological innovation, industry organization itself has become more flexible, mirroring in part the Italian model of dispersed manufacturing units balanced by centralized marketing structures. Another salient feature is the sharply increased use of sub-contracting.

Paralleling these developments, intra-EC trade had by and large

64

grown to high levels by 1985. For textiles, where Germany is the intra-EC export leader, it was about a quarter of total Community consumption. For man-made fibres, a highly integrated sector whose export leader is the UK, almost half of EC consumption was met by intra-Community trade. But it is a different story for the clothing sub-sector, where cross-frontier trade is only half the level achieved for textiles. Labour-intensive, clothing production has shifted in part to low-wage developing countries. Intra-EC trade is led by the Italian industry. By and large trade in textiles and clothing continues to be restricted by a system of import quotas distributed between individual EC countries.

Further cost effects of removing residual barriers
These national quotas (granted under Article 115 of the Rome Treaty) necessitate border controls, have a segmenting effect on the common market, and are clearly incompatible with the aim of complete elimination of intra-Community frontiers by 1992. Be that as it may, most producers interviewed for the research find few problems living with residual barriers, eg. labelling requirements, country of origin problems, differing VAT rates, time lost at border crossings. For dynamic companies, selling on the domestic market or abroad makes little difference. Indeed, one Italian firm said it had greater problems selling to southern Italy than to Germany or France. The prevailing picture, at least from industry's standpoint, is that integration of the Community market is near completion.

As a result, the removal of the remaining trade barriers is only likely to have marginal effects on intra-EC trade flows. Ensuing direct cost reductions, it is estimated, might be around 0.2% of unit costs. A further saving of about 0.5% might be ascribable to additional economies of scale beyond those already attained. But there is limited potential for this – in the textiles sector because of the existing degree of specialization, and for clothing because production does not lend itself easily to mechanization and automation. Gains yet to be realized lie more with marketing than with output.

Outlook for consumer prices
For textiles and man-made fibres, in which price competition is already fierce, further cost reductions may nevertheless be expected to run through to consumer prices.

The story is different for clothing, which is a sector characterized by highly differentiated products and where price is not necessarily the main factor affecting consumer behaviour. Indeed price differences, which in part reflect sharply differing consumer tastes

65

between EC countries, can be as much as 200% for some articles. Some businessmen contacted said they set prices for the EC in a discretionary range of about 10% of the net final price.

Factors like this make it difficult to assess the effect on consumer prices of any reductions in production costs pursuant to removal of trade barriers. It is quite conceivable, for example, that reduction in production prices might be absorbed to an extent by the retail system, where mark-ups often account for more than half of the final consumer price.

Pharmaceuticals

Overview
The pharmaceuticals sector presents something of a special case, its products being irretrievably linked to the sensitive issue of human health. For consumers, strict control on drug safety and quality is imperative. This is a concern for the public authorities who are also directly involved because they foot around 50% on average of the pharmaceutical bill. Industry, on the other hand, has to finance increasingly heavy investments, mainly in R&D, the return on which is neither short-term nor sure.

This mingling of public and private interests makes the pharmaceuticals market highly characteristic – one in which typically the final consumer does not pay for the product, in which the producer is not free to fix his product price, and in which government is simultaneously the principal paying agent and price controller. Needless to say, the sector is highly regulated, with two areas of regulation – the market registration procedure for new products, and price controls – being the most important from the standpoint of the European market.

The time and funding requirements for pharmaceutical research are becoming steadily greater, and not just because of the efforts needed to get new drugs admitted to differing national markets and of the costs created by the potential for discrimination in pricing procedures (see below). The chief cause is that traditional medical research is reaching its limits, and its successor, the commercial exploitation of biotechnologies, is in expensive infancy. Only the largest of firms can make the estimated Ecu 75m outlay needed to bring each new chemical entity (NCE) to the market, after 8-12 years of testing and evaluation.

Faced with these facts, EC policy is seeking to build a framework which discourages government favours for local producers and stimulates the industry's R&D efforts by freer competition. The opportunities created by this will be for EC governments and companies to seize, otherwise the main gains of market integration will be for extra-EC firms. With the maintenance of high levels of public health in the EC linked significantly to activities of the Community's own pharmaceuticals industry, it may not be in the interests of EC patients to become unduly dependent on research conducted outside the Community.

Registration procedures biggest focus for cost savings
Admission of new products to national markets is subject to registration procedures to ensure that a drug is safe, effective and of adequate quality before it is put on sale.

Despite action by the Community, considerable problems still face companies as a result of lengthy and differing drug registration procedures between EC countries. Over the last two decades, EC initiatives have led to the convergence of the requirements made by national regulatory authorities. As a result there are few differences in technical standards (eg. all EC countries accept test evidence obtained elsewhere in the Community), and a uniform 120-day decision has been agreed.

In practice, however, the story is different. There remain substantial differences between countries – eg. varying methods of evaluating evidence, and above all considerable delays in processing applications. Currently only France approaches the 120-day limit for drug registration procedures. Germany and the UK take about two years, and Italy and Spain three or more. A single European registration agency could be considered as a way of easing the present situation by helping to overcome differences in national practice. Industry is concerned that such a structure might be too burdensome. The key issue remains the speed of registration, which should be improved.

Delays in registration trigger a range of costs. Losses in revenues suffered by companies forced to wait over the agreed 120-day limit are estimated at between Ecu 100–175m. Working capital tied up by such delays is calculated at a further Ecu 20–28m. Multiple registration is an additional problem and, based on the extra staff employed by the major companies to handle it, is estimated at Ecu 40–55m. Adding these items up, the total cost of non-Europe due to differences in registration practices lies in a spread of 0.5%–0.8% of EC industry costs.

Pricing procedures
All EC countries have measures to control public expenditure on pharmaceuticals. These measures, differing from one country to the other, involve controls both on prices for new products and on

changes in prices of drugs already on the market, as well as on their reimbursement by social security systems.

Research has thrown up definite evidence that these national pricing systems may operate with discriminatory bias. Prices and profit margins in several member states depend on the scale and nature of a company's local activities. Local performance requirements of this sort clearly operate in favour of the domestic manufacturer, while involving the foreign firm in excessive decentralisation of key functions. Drug production, being essentially a two-phase process, involves manufacture of so-called active ingredients at a limited number of sites, and then the conversion of these into dosage form, frequently in a variety of sites. Decentralization of this latter process is, according to the research, often a result of pressure exerted by host governments during price negotiations. Bowing to such pressures can mean sacrificing economies of scale.

To discourage this distorted use of national pricing systems, the Commission has opted for a gradualist approach. The draft Community directive on price controls, proposed in 1986, seeks to give the manufacturer greater certainty on how national pricing systems operate by requiring them to be more transparent.

The research considers some alternative scenarios, which might develop in the wake of the transparency directive, based on different degrees of concentration realized in response to an easing of local performance requirements. Although necessarily tentative, they suggest the potential for savings in operating costs which the directive might produce. If prices remained unchanged, the firm's operating surplus might be increased by between 7% and 14%. Alternatively, if passed on in their entirety to the consumer, the result could be to reduce expenditure on pharmaceuticals by between 1.3% and 2.4% on average.

Outlook

By and large, the research tends to support the view that Community legislation aimed at further freeing of the European pharmaceuticals market could release considerable resources. These could be used to increase company margins, thus improving the capacity of firms to innovate, and to reduce drug prices, thus reducing public expenditure.

PART II
THE 1992 OPPORTUNITY: THE GAINS IN PROSPECT

8 From market costs to economic benefits – a twin-track approach for estimating overall gains

The costs caused by European market fragmentation have been highlighted in the preceding examples, which illustrate the scale of market barriers and how they impact on selected sectors of business.

As indicated in Part I, these costs take various shapes but are essentially of two types: those which will be eliminated immediately once barriers are removed; and those, much more sizeable, which are economic inefficiencies that will only be unravelled and replaced by more dynamic practices over time under the competitive pressures of the integrated EC market. Looked at another way, these costs are the expression in negative terms of the benefits that will emerge for the Community economy as a whole after the barriers are eliminated. But to gauge these overall benefits, a more general analysis than that pursued in Part I becomes necessary. This is the purpose of Part II.

Order-of-magnitude estimates of the benefits to be had from the European home market of the 1990s are outlined, using two distinct but complementary approaches, in respectively chapters 9 and 10. Use of these two methods – respectively a micro-economic and macro-economic approach – was dictated by the novelty of the conceptual challenge to be overcome in making the estimate, and by the inevitable unevenness in the empirical data on which it is based. This in turn made cross-checking of the results, rendered possible by employing two approaches, all the more necessary. As will be seen, the two estimates converge on broadly similar – and economically very substantial – levels of gain for the European economy.

A word, for the general reader, to demystify the economic jargon, and briefly situate the two approaches.

The micro-economic estimate   This first approach (Chapter 9) takes as its starting point the impact of removing non-tariff barriers on the individual actors of the Community economy, and seeks to establish what general benefits accrue to them – be they companies, consumers or government – as a result of the supply-side shock given by market integration.

Viewed from this standpoint, highlights of the 1992 picture

include a substantial gain for consumers ('consumer surplus') as prices drop and product choice and quality increase under the impact of open competition. Producers face a more mixed outlook. In the short term, profits (particularly those resulting from monopoly or protected positions) may be squeezed. But in the longer run, business as a whole is expected to respond to the new competitive climate by making various adjustments – eg. scaling up production ('economies of scale of production'), gaining experience of how to produce most efficiently ('economies of scale of learning' or 'learning curve effect'), eliminating management inefficiencies ('X-inefficiency' to the economist), and by improved capacity to innovate. Gains from these and other adjustments, when netted out, lead to an increase in the Community's 'net economic welfare'. This increase is its 'net welfare gain'.[16]

The macro-economic estimate   Chapter 10 looks at how the supply-side shock given by removal of barriers will reverberate on the main indicators of the Community economy – indicators like gross domestic product, inflation, employment, public budgets and the external position.

The process is in essence simple. It starts with the lowering of production costs and with gains in productivity which will result from EC market integration. The ensuing price reductions will in turn have an important knock-on effect on the main mechanisms of the macro-economy. They will increase purchasing power; change the competitive positions of individual EC countries with each other and of the Community with the outside world; they will provide the basis for a durable attack on unemployment; stimulate demand yet reduce inflation; in short, they will provide an entirely new outlook – and trajectory – for economic growth between now and the end of the century.

These beneficial effects provide a further and substantial impact. They give the managers of the general economy – governments – much greater leeway for measures that would magnify the primary gains of market integration into benefits much larger still.

A final introductory point. This is that the gains forecast for the European economy will not appear as if by divine intervention. Realizing the potential that is on offer presupposes a robustly positive response to the supply-side opportunity by business and government. 1992 is not simply a date. It is a programme, and a strategy.

9 In quest of Europe's lost 200 billions – a micro-economic analysis of gains from market integration

The competitive vista of 1992

A dramatically new environment awaits consumers and producers alike in the integrated Community market post-1992. As shown in Part I, the removal of a whole range of non-tarrif barriers – eg. frontier red-tape, closed public procurement, a plethora of differing product standards – leads to an immediate downward impact on costs. But this is merely the primary effect, and thus only a minor part of the story explaining the environment of the European home market in the next decade.

Much more substantial gains will be generated by completion of the EC internal market. Its attainment means not just the simple elimination of constraints sapping effective business performance, but above all a new and pervasive competitive climate. One in which the players of the European economy – manufacturing and service companies, and consumers of their output – can exploit new opportunities and better use available resources.

Four major consequences may be expected from the combined impact of the elimination of barriers and the subsequent boost to competition:

- significant reduction in costs, thanks to improved exploitation by companies of economies of scale in production and business organization;
- improved efficiency within companies, widespread industrial reorganization, and a situation where prices move downward toward production costs under the pressure of more competitive markets;
- new patterns of competition between entire industries and reallocation of resources as, in home market conditions, real comparative advantages play the determining role in market success;
- increased innovation, new business processes and products generated by the dynamics of the internal market.

Of course these various effects will not occur simultaneously.

They will be spread over differing time-spans. But their overall impact is clear. They will increase the competitivity of business and the general economic welfare of the consumer.

For consumers: an unqualified bonus

Put simply, consumers will be better off. Be they private individuals or intermediary businesses, the outlook is unreservedly good. They will no longer be confronted, as in today's Community, with enormous price differences depending on their country of residence. Apart from inevitable variations in prices linked to inherent characteristics of a particular product or service, European consumers will be paying a similar price for the same item. And, as the item will tend to be produced in the cheapest way, the level of this price will be on a downward journey. There will also be greater consumer choice, as market integration and increased competition lead to differentiated products as well as economies of scale.

For companies: the challenge of success, but an end to national soft options

For firms the era of the national soft option will be over. But for companies able to scale up their performance to the demands of increased competition, the outlook for sales and profits is dynamic. The boost given to competition by increased intra-EC trade will stimulate the competitivity of European businesses in three ways:

1. Lower input costs Companies will be able to cover their basic requirements – labour, capital, plant and components – more cost-effectively. This cost improvement in production factors stems directly from lower prices for many intermediate goods and services as well as from general market integration, and leads in turn to more rational factors, allocation between firms, sectors and countries.

2. Responsiveness of profits to competition Profits could clearly be squeezed by Europe's competitive renewal, but for high performance firms they may improve as a result of gains in business' internal efficiency. Two main factors will have a bullish effect on company margins. First, the increased dimension of the market means higher utilization rates for production capacity and possible expansion of capital stock, and enables reorganization and concentration of business activities. Second, improved internal cost controls should reduce overheads, lead to 'best practice' production techniques and, by sharpening the demands on it, strengthen the quality of European corporate management. From the profit standpoint, EC integration gives management a supply side shock – a market-sent opportunity

74

to optimize existing resources, modernize plant, and to promote new activities and new ways of organizing work.

3. *A spur to innovation* Market integration brings with it a number of factors giving European firms the chance to regain technological leadership. Among these factors: European market liberalization and growth; the removal of market entry barriers (eg. standards); the creation of new companies, particularly in high tech sectors; and the rapid development of cross-frontier business cooperation for R&D. Only when European companies regain this leadership can they call the shots – or, in the language of economics, go from being 'price-takers' to 'price-makers'.

In short, strengthening European competitivity leads, so to speak, to the reconquest of the European market. Failure to meet the demands of competitivity does not mean that the challenges of the European market will not be mastered. They will. But not by Europeans.

The successive phases of benefit from market integration
The gate to market integration is the elimination of non-tariff barriers. Once unlocked, the gate opens on to a space much larger than expected, and it is the interplay of newly-liberated factors in this extended space that provides the full picture of the dynamic gains to be had from the process. The cause-and-effect circuit of micro-economic gains resultant on market integration is given in the flow-chart on page p.76.

Chart 9.1 traces, first, how the removal of non-tariff barriers leads to a direct reduction of initial costs and, given stable competitive conditions, to lower prices. It also shows how barrier removal increases competitive pressures which, in turn, trigger more price reductions and pull prices down towards costs via an impact on profit margins.

This chapter looks at the various aspects of this interplay. The analysis has had to overcome a range of complex problems including limited EC-wide data and methodological challenges. Nonetheless, using the most prudent of hypotheses, the overall result is impressive, and is detailed below in successive sections whose main themes are now rapidly outlined.

On the basis of the findings illustrated in Part I, it was established that the removal of non-tariff barriers leads to direct reductions in the costs and prices for goods and services for final consumption, and also for intermediary items, and that these savings then lead to growth in domestic and international demand. Demand growth in turn enables increases in the volume of output and loosens the

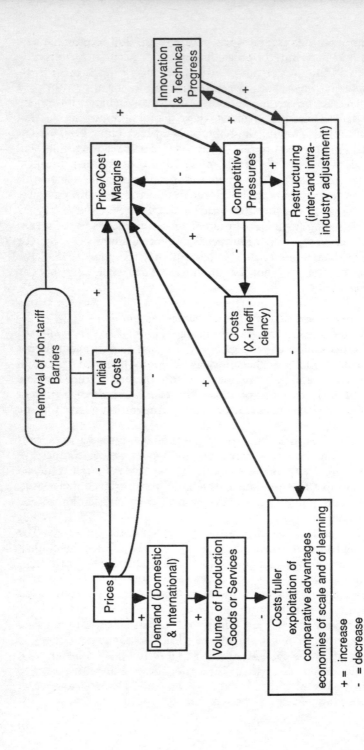

Chart 9.1 Flow-chart of micro-economic effects triggered by EC market integration

+ = increase
- = decrease

constraints which, hitherto, have hindered the full exploitation of economies of scale and the 'learning curve' effect (companies learning to do things more efficiently as a result of doing them more often). *Section 1* examines these potential cost savings.

Beyond gains in economies of scale and learning, are those pursuant to business rationalization and the elimination of sub-optimal production units – gains which come about in response to the new competitive stimuli injected by the integrated market. *Section 2* looks at the impact of these stimuli on price levels and company profits.

Section 3, using two separate approaches for analysing the same phenomena, calculates the likely spread of benefits to be expected from the completion of the internal market. These benefits are expressed in terms of improvements in the economic welfare of consumers and producers. The dynamic effects of EC-wide competition on Europe's innovation and technology performance are outlined in *Section 4*.

While some of the gains from the internal market will occur almost automatically, most require changes in the behaviour of the economy's main players to achieve maximum impact. *Section 5* outlines the new strategic challenges facing companies. These challenges will only be taken up by companies if they have credible assurances that competititive behaviour is adequately policed. A firm competition policy is part and parcel of the European home market of the 1990s (*Section 6*).

1 Economies of scale and experience: outlook for business
Increased trade and sharper competition triggered by market integration will enable firms to make savings linked to larger-scale production. Empirical studies show that, for the sectors considered (see Chapters 6 and 7), the greater the opening to trade, the greater the move towards the size needed to achieve the necessary economies of scale to compete. Compound benefits result. It is not merely the productivity of transformed resources that is enhanced: the additional economies of scale for the extra output for export allows a lowering of cost on the total amount of existing production.

The analysis here had to take account of three complicating factors:

a) *Potential gains vary significantly by industry*: the expected reductions in production costs resultant on economies of scale are of the order of 1% for sectors like petroleum products, but reach a spread of 3%–6% for heavy electrical equipment and means of transport other than cars.

b) *Diverse applications of economies of scale*: in addition to production, they may be possible for business organization, marketing, finance, and R&D. In some of these cases, economies of scale are difficult to quantify.

c) *Adjustments to scale take different forms*: there are two main types, with varying time-spans for their achievement. First, more intensive use of existing capacity in response to increased demand for the output of differing industries in differing countries, depending on their comparative advantage. Second, restructuring within each industry in each country, involving the disappearance of the smallest or least efficient companies, or their concentration, and the development of new and greater specialization.

Taking just manufacturing industries, the calculations show that the cost savings to be had from economies of scale for production would be around Ecu 60 billion. The vast majority of these savings (80%) would derive from restructuring.

There is no doubt that this estimate, large as it may seem, understates overall gains from this source. It takes no account of economies of scale in areas other than production, and it does not include the service sector of the economy. Nor are the so-called learning-curve effects part of the calculation. These can be very significant, as studies have repeatedly shown. It is now established that the accumulation over time of the production of goods and services has, through learning acquired 'on the job', triggered considerable drops in the cost of producing additional units. Thus, given a doubling of overall production, unit costs for supplementary production will drop an average of 10% in refining and in car manufacturing, and 20% in aircraft manufacture.[17] Inasmuch as the completion of the internal market will tend to increase the scale of production and growth in demand, the accompanying gains for companies from using their accumulated production experience seem certain to be considerable.

2 Price levels and profit margins : business and the supply-side shock

For a given product, competitive pressures tend to trigger a downward convergence of prices. This factor in turn lowers profit margins to the extent that they have been artificially sustained above competitive levels. Moreover, the adjustment of prices to supply and demand pressures is generally greater and quicker in a competitive environment. Market integration in Europe will lead to substantial gains of this type.

Price differences
A starting point of the benefit analysis here is the observable price differences presently obtaining for a given product between EC countries. Such differences, of course, cannot be entirely ascribed to the non-Europe factor, indeed some may occur within national markets. They may in part reflect certain fairly immutable characteristics – transport costs, the inherent advantages of certain locations, variations in consumer tastes, custom and culture. Nonetheless, such 'natural barriers' cannot alone explain the size of the before-tax differences in prices, nor the fact that country-to-country discrepancies are much greater than those occurring within a national market (see Table 9.1 for a price comparison in the home electronics sector).

Taking the situation across the board, the general before-tax price variation from the Community average in 1985 was 15.2% for consumer goods and 12.4% for capital equipment. These global averages conceal much greater price dispersion for individual items, eg. tea (27%); ladies' linen and hosiery (31%); glass and crockery (21%); books (49%); boilermaking equipment (22%). Examples of price differences in the service sector (tax inclusive) appear even more spectacular : telephone and telegraph services (50%); electrical repairs (42%); road and rail transport (28%).

Such differences witness forcibly to the existence of artificial barriers stopping the natural play of arbitrage between member state markets. For illustrations of the particular impact of specific non-

Table 9.1   National price differences compared with intra-EC differences – the case of home electronics in Germany

	F.R. Germany*	Community**
Compact-disc players	10.6	14.9
Radio recorders	7.3	16.2
Turntables	9.6	10.8
Video recorders	5.7	13.2
Cam recorders	6.8	11.3
Video cassettes	5.7	13.3
Washing machines	3.3	13.4
Colour TV	6.4	13.5

* Source: Institut für Angewandte Verbraucherforschung (IFAV). The coefficient of variation has been calculated on the basis of average prices in major German towns
** Source: Bureau Europeén des Unions des consommateurs (BEUC) and Eurostat (last two products). The number of Member States taken into account varies according to the product

tariff barriers, see for example Chapter 3 (public procurement) and Chapters 6 and 7 for instances of their sectoral impact.

Price differences are reinforced by restrictive competitive behaviour and the market structures for certain goods and services in certain countries. A particularly striking instance is financial services, where cartelistic practices in some countries result in large price differentials in the EC, eg. for interest rates on consumer credits (see also Table 6.1). Studies carried out in Britain and France show just how substantial are the losses in efficiency linked to monopoly power in certain industries. There is, moreover, an irresistible correlation (more than 80%) between the sectors for whose products there are large price differences between EC countries and those where industrial power is concentrated.

The European home market will do much to put a stop to this sort of business. By liberating cross-frontier trade flows, it will create the permanent prospect and credible threat of new market entrants coming in to undermine non-competitive prices. Not only actual but potential competition will be reinforced – the door, once opened, will be permanently ajar. Prices, within the limits imposed by 'natural barriers', will move remorselessly nearer to costs.

Profit margins
One expected consequence of strengthened competition is a squeeze on those profit margins which are simply due to enterprises cashing in on monopoly or protected positions. At the same time, competitive European companies will reap considerable cost savings which, despite the downward impact of lowering prices, will keep profits buoyant. They will be further boosted by their strengthened capacity to take on foreign competition for global markets, and by the structural increase in European demand which will be theirs for the taking.

The positive outlook for lower company costs, reflecting both the direct impact of barrier removal and the subsequent exploitation of economies of scale and learning, has already been outlined both in Part I and in section 1 of this chapter. Production costs will come down for goods and services for final consumption and also for intermediary goods. The reduction in these input costs will have a radiating effect throughout the European business economy.

These are by no means the only gains in prospect for companies. It is widely accepted that, without the discipline of market pressures, firms rapidly become victims of ineffective cost control, under-utilized resources, out-of-date technology, inefficient internal operations – in short, bad management. Inefficiencies of this sort have been given prominence in various studies, which estimate that internal reorganization can alone lead to savings in company overheads of more than 10%.

In sum, EC market integration heralds a prospect of rich pickings to be earned, not inherited. For European companies prepared to seize the competitive gauntlet, operational rationalization and internal reorganization will lead to greater competitivity and a durably strong bottom line.

3 Estimating the gains in European economic welfare

Estimating the overall gains for the European economy from EC market integration is a challenging process. Two distinct methods of evaluation were used. In simple terms, these two methods, briefly explained below,[18] may be described as :

- a price convergence approach
- a welfare gains approach.

Price convergence approach

This method is based on the price dispersion between EC countries summarized in the preceding section. Its starting point is that completion of the internal market will have a different impact on prices depending on the characteristics of the industry concerned. Thus it is assumed that price differences in sectors with few or weak non-tariff barriers and a high level of import penetration (eg. man-made fibres, optical instruments, dairy products) are a consequence of factors not by and large ascribable to the absence of a European home market. By contrast, the opposite is the case for sectors with high barriers and low penetration (office automation, railway rolling stock, telecom equipment and services, pharmaceuticals, etc). A characteristic common to many of these sectors (see Part I) is the predominant purchasing role played by the public authorities.

With this as its starting point, the following approach was adopted. First, for sectors with low non-tariff barriers, the assumption was made that such price peaks as there are will be brought down to the Community average under the pressure of market integration.

Second, for sectors protected by high barriers, the assumption is that integration will lead to a price level equal to the average of the prices obtaining in the two EC countries with the lowest levels at the moment. This, it should be stressed, is a conservative basis on which to calculate gains, since it is perfectly possible that the lowest prices in today's EC market will, as a result of cost savings brought on by intensified competition, be reduced.

The aggregate drop in price levels is one way of measuring the overall gains from EC market integration. It reflects cost reductions directly stemming from barrier removal and impacting not just on the trade of goods but on their production; indirect cost reductions triggered by the better use of economies of scale and by improved internal company organization; and finally, the unfettering of business' competitive powers in an integrated market of continental proportions.

Using this approach and assuming that present output remains unchanged, total savings from the drop in prices is of the order of 4.8% of gross domestic product.[19] It should be stressed that these savings do not express the EC's welfare gains in full, for they take no account of the rises in overall output resultant on lower prices, nor of the probability that the lowest prices presently observed will themselves fall as industry is more fully rationalized at the European level.

Welfare gains approach
The second method covers this omission. It seeks to translate the available empirical data into figures expressing the overall economic advantage, or welfare gains, for the Community's consumers and producers as a result of market integration.

Two types of gain are to be distinguished. The first is the gain for consumers (or 'consumer surplus') stemming from lower prices and larger purchases. This corresponds in part to a drop in profit for producers faced with new competition. The size of this drop has to be deducted from the level of the consumer surplus.

The second type of gain is more substantial because the reductions are in costs linked to operational inefficiencies which are a pure gain for the economic community as a whole. Since this gain affects output across the board, it is clearly large in size. Thus, while the removal of tariff barriers (involving drops in government revenue), for example, leads to fairly small gains in overall economic welfare, the gain from the elimination of non-tariff barriers is of substantial economic significance.

The calculations made to evaluate overall economic welfare gains have taken account of these distinctions. This was done with the aid of theoretical models for international trade analysis. These have been given greater sophistication of late, enabling accurate analysis of certain aspects of trade not adequately treated by traditional international trade theory. They take into account, for example, phenomena like economies of scale, product differentiation and imperfect competitive behaviour where suppliers exercise a certain control over prices. Applying these models to some ten industrial sectors in five country groups (France, Germany, Italy, the United Kingdom and the Benelux group), the authors[20] conclude that the lowering of non-tariff barriers improves EC economic welfare, thanks to growth in EC trade and output, to lower unit production costs and to more diversified products. There would be further welfare benefits from European integration in the medium and long term, according to this theory. These reflect reductions in cost as a result of industrial restructuring, and a narrowing of the gap between prices and costs in the wake of the curtailment of monopoly power.

The significance of these exercises in theoretical simulation lies not so much in their end result as in their identification of the relative size of the causes of gains in economic welfare. On this their message is clear. The more the European market is integrated, the greater the contribution of indirect gains (derived from business restructuring and intensified competition) as opposed to direct gains (largely reflected by increased intra-EC trade). According to this approach, indirect gains would constitute around 60% of the Community's overall benefit in economic welfare.

The total estimate of economic gain to the EC, using these various methods, is situated in a spread around a mid-point of over Ecu 200 billion (for the twelve EC member states, expressed in 1988 prices). The range represents between 4.3% and 6.4% of the Community's gross domestic product in 1988.

Table 9.2 outlines the potential welfare gains for consumers and producers. It presents the aggregate beneficial effects from reductions in costs and prices for each of the four successive phases in the micro-economic analysis of the process of welfare gains.

The calculation set out in Table 9.2 has been carried out in four distinct steps:

1 *Step 1*: the removal of barriers which directly affect intra-EC trade, essentially customs formalities and related delays (for details, see Chapter 2);

2 *Step 2*: the effects of removing barriers to production (ie. not simply intra-EC trade): these are barriers which hinder foreign market entrants and thus the free play of competition. Examples include protective public procurement (see Chapter 3), divergent national standards and regulatory diversity (Chapters 4 & 5), and restrictions on services (Chapter 6) and on manufacturing (Chapter 7). Such obstacles do much more than hinder trade. In limiting the impact of competitive pressures, they sustain excess costs and over-pricing.

3 *Step 3*: represents the cost reductions achieved by businesses though exploiting more fully potential economies of scale

Table 9.2   Potential gains in economic welfare for the EC resulting from completion of the internal market

	Billions Ecu	% of Gdp
Step 1		
Gains from removal of barriers affecting trade	8–9	0.2–0.3
Step 2		
Gains from removal of barriers affecting overall production	57–71	2.0–2.4
Gains from removing barriers (sub-total)	65–80	2.2–2.7
Step 3		
Gains from exploiting economies of scale more fully	61	2.1
Step 4		
Gains from intensified competition reducing business inefficiencies and monopoly profits	46	1.6
Gains from market integration (sub-total)	62*-107	2.1*–3.7
Total		
– for 7 Member States at 1985 prices	127–187	4.3–6.4
– for 12 Member States at 1988 prices	174–258	4.3–6.4
– mid-point of above	216	5.3

* This alternative estimate for the sum of steps 3 and 4 cannot be broken down between the two steps.

Source: Commission of EC, study of Directorate-General for Economic and Financial Affairs, op. cit.

Notes: The ranges for cetain lines represent the results of using alternative sources of information and methodologies. The seven Member States (Germany, France, Italy, United Kingdom, Benelux) account for 88% of the Gdp of the EC twelve. Extrapolation of the results in terms of the same share of Gdp for the seven and twelve Member States is not likely to over-estimate the total for the twelve. The detailed figures in the table relate only to the seven Member States because the underlying studies mainly covered those countries.

(Section 1 above). These gains arise in part in the short-run as increases in production allow fixed investment costs to be covered by larger sales volumes. To a much more important extent, however, they accrue in the longer run as companies and production units are restructured and get closer to the most efficient possible scales of production.

4   *Step 4*: represents other gains in efficiency due to intensified pressures of competition (see Section 2 above). These gains may, for example, concern administrative overhead costs, over-manning at all levels, and inefficient management of inventories. Evidence from a variety of sources suggests that these kinds of efficiency

gains can be of considerable importance. In addition, where monopoly profits exist as a result of market protection, they will be reduced or eliminated, and thus offer gains for consumers through price reductions.

This aggregate outcome, which emphasizes if need be the political and economic imperative of the White Paper programme, is in a way still not the complete picture. It fails to take full account of the overall dynamics to be unleashed by the creation of a European home market. Notable among these are new business strategies and technical innovation.

4 Market dynamics and technological progess

For companies, costs and prices are increasingly just two of the components of their competitive strategy for the 1990s – indeed as of now. Today, more than ever before, is witness to the emergence of more telling competitive weaponry. Business' capacity to develop new forms of organization, to penetrate new geographical markets, to invent new products and new processes – these are the stuff of which competitive edge is made. Comparative advantage is no longer seen as divine inheritance, nor are market structures and rivals' behaviour set in tablets of stone.

These 'non-price' factors, central to competitive business strategies, are dynamic and subject to continual change. And among these factors, the role of innovation is crucial. It is the key to the revitalization of traditional sectors, able to transform certain areas of textiles, for example, into high-performance industries, and it is the *sine qua non* for lasting success in the rapidly expanding high technology sectors.

The competitive pressures accompanying EC market integration will impact positively on technical progress, both as regards product and process invention and the ensuing innovations. And the capacity to innovate will itself further fuel these pressures. So much is clear. It is less easy, however, to measure the effects. But some signposts in this rapidly changing landscape may serve as a guide.

Worthy of note is the fact that large firms conduct no more research, proportionately speaking, than smaller firms. Nor are they responsible for a proportionately larger number of innovations.[21] The enlargement of market dimension and the restructuring of Europe's productive potential should enable many firms to undertake and finance costly and risky R&D projects, and to market the new products and processes emerging from them. Even more important, perhaps, the sharpening of cross-border competition – resultant on the reduction of market entry barriers, the creation of new firms and on the greater mobility of researchers – will intensify innovations and accelerate their spread.

The positive link between innovation and competition is confirmed in, among others, a recent study.[22] Innovations are more numerous in industries with low market entry barriers and high production growth. The positive impact of market integration on business innovation will be most acute in high technology sectors and in those with a strong outlook for growth in demand.

A virtuous circle
These are precisely the sectors in which Europe's loss of market shares since the beginning of the 1980s has been most marked, and where a new competitive thrust is most needed. The completion of the internal market could thus trigger a virtuous circle, where greater competition stimulates European innovation and innovation in turn stimulates European competitivity.

This type of competition has of course nothing to do with the textbook version. But it has a lot to do with the reality of strategic rivalry played out between a limited number of firms in a situation of uncertainty. Seen against this background of oligopoly struggles, it appears that the EC's pattern of cooperative behaviour for R&D, coupled with tough competition in the end market, might further the general welfare more than totally non-cooperative behaviour. This leads to consideration of the role expected of the economy's main players – Europe's corporate citizens – as they move to realize the potential gains of the European home market.

5 Business strategies for the European home market
It is clear that the benefits expected from market integration will not appear at the wave of a wand. To bring them about many changes are needed, not least the gearing up of business strategies to meet the new market's greater challenges.

Indications of how companies intend to adjust to the 1992 environment are provided in the business survey conducted in 1987.[23] They seem to envisage three main types of action: measures aimed at restructuring and improving productivity, growing recourse to international link-ups, especially for R&D, and penetration of new markets.

Company restructuring Restructuring can occur internally or externally. Internal restructuring occurs, for example, when companies rationalize their activities, refocusing them around a main line of business and dropping areas foreign to it, or when they move to extend their penetration of the enlarged home market. Examples of external restructuring are more visible. They include take-overs and mergers enabling improved exploitation of economies of scale, access to new geographical markets, and a greater division of labour between the various parts of the European market. Such operations can help companies attain a truly European dimension and thus escape from the narrow logic of the 'national champion'.

Statistics for 1985-86[24] show for EC companies an increase in the numbers of take-overs and asset mergers they undertook both cross-border in the Community and with non-EC partners, at the expense of purely national link-ups. (All the same, in 1986 nearly two-thirds of mergers and majority share links were still taking place behind national borders.) As regards transnational operations, intra-EC mergers were nearly twice as numerous as those involving non-EC partners. Worthy of remark is that majority share acquisitions were dominated by large-size companies. Around 50% of these acquisitions were made by companies with turnover in excess of Ecu 1,000m.

For small and medium-sized companies, attainment of the home market should create the occasion for consolidation of often sub-optimal units geared to meeting the demands of narrow national product markets.

At the same time, a cautionary note needs to be struck. Successful business restructuring depends on a variety of other factors – new modes of company management and organization, the training of management and its international mobility, as well as its openness to social dialogue. Various studies suggest that there is considerable room for progress in these areas.[25]

Inter-company cooperative link-ups The total number of newly-created joint subsidiaries remains fairly stable.[26] Such operations mounted cross-border between EC firms remain a minority (24.7% of the total), less than those involving a non-EC partner (33.3%), while purely national operations continue strongest (42%). A similar picture emerges for minority participations. More generally, planned cooperative agreements run into a list of obstacles which is as impressive as the resultant failure rate. On top of the inherent problems faced by companies in joining forces (getting the right balance between partners, setting up cost-effective management, achieving fair distribution of the fruits of cooperation, etc.) come a series of further hurdles linked in the main to business law and industry regulation.

Seven such barriers have particular impact (see diagram below).[27]

Costliest of these barriers for trans-border cooperative start-ups and management appear to be the near absence of relevant European company and tax law. They include the problems of EC-wide tax consolidation in fiscally disparate environments and of cross-frontier intra-company pricing. Obstacles to the mobility of human resources linked to differing social security laws are also shown to be significant. Divergent national standards, meanwhile, make heavy inroads into R&D budgets.

The overriding paradox which emerges is that international co-operative link-ups between EC partner firms have up to now proved less frequent than those with a non-EC participant. The scope for correcting this balance is considerable once the barriers come down. At the same time, links with non-EC participants are also very useful for European competitiveness and might be more used as a platform for attacking world markets (as well as the non-EC partner's penetration of Community markets). Thus once a European company has reached a threshold of competitive performance thanks to cost savings inherent in economies of scale and learning, and a level of strategic capacity thanks to its marketing, R&D and human resource power, it is well placed to penetrate foreign markets through an alliance with a local company.

Market entry is a key factor influencing the success of new business strategies. Chief among the traditional sources of American business dynamism is the perpetual flux of market entries and exits, providing a steady renewal of market players. This elixir of industrial rejuvenation is at its most potent in the high technology sectors where newcomers to the market make a disproportionately high contribution to new products and processes. Europe presents a starkly contrasting picture. More often than not, large established firms monopolize the stage thanks to privileged links with the national public powers.

But, with the new impulses of trade and competition released by the removal of non-tariff barriers, market entry opportunities will multiply for new firms with new ideas and new competitive strengths. The prospect of the renewal of the Community's industrial tissue encompasses small and medium-sized companies as well. Cooperation between such firms will be encouraged by more open market entry, aiding them also to enter the competition for global markets.

Global competition and European comparative advantage
Of course, from the opposite standpoint, emerges the challenge posed to European companies by the rivalry they will face from non-Community companies on their enlarged home market. The expectation must be that this challenge will be sharpened as market entry barriers recede. Recent performance of EC firms in competing with their Japanese and American rivals for world and European markets is far from brilliant. Since the start of the 1980s, Community business has seen an erosion of its position on many world manufacturing markets, while its two major competitors have gained. The Japanese and American advantage is particularly pronounced in advanced technology sectors like electrical and electronic goods, office automation equipment and data-processing. EC companies have resisted better on European markets, but even so there is a real danger that in sectors like pharmaceuticals, foodstuffs and certain high tech areas the main beneficiaries of market integration could be non-Community – be they American, Swiss, Japanese or from among the newly industrialized countries.

This challenge can be met by the right European business strategies. Various factors will be key to the success of the European riposte – full exploitation of innovation capacities; the 'first-mover advantage' for locally-established companies; full use of 'best-practice' production processes to consolidate the first-mover market advantage; close, durable and costly-to-replace relations between local suppliers and clients, etc.[28] It is in these and other ways that European specificity, and thus European comparative advantage, can assert itself. An ever more potent weapon in the arsenal of competitive conflict, Europe-wide standards (for products, processes, financial reporting, information etc.) are an essential lever both for prising open national markets and then welding them together through technological alliances. Of great importance to such alliances are EC-sponsored R&D programmes like Esprit which, way beyond their monetary significance, are a crucial focus for fusing cross-frontier innovation and business synergies.

6 Maintaining fair competition

But companies mounting the strategies demanded by the 1992 challenge need the certainty of clear rules, firmly enforced, for playing the European home market game.

Full realization of the positive effects of integration will indeed depend in large part on the maintenance of open competition. Assured of this, companies will be more prepared to exploit new opportunities. Gains in productivity and lower costs will throughput to lower prices, better quality and greater product choice. In short, overall economic welfare will improve.

In this new and blustery climate, however, there is a good chance that some of the economy's players will seek various forms of shelter from competitive reinvigoration. This happened following the removal of tariff barriers, and it is to be expected that the Community's authorities will face multiple strategems developed by private and public actors to cushion the competitive impact on them, eg.:

- the creation of dominant positions potentially leading to abuses, like barriers to new entrants to the market, market sharing, and discriminatory behaviour;
- greater recourse to public interventionism, whether direct or indirect, aimed at artificially sustaining national champions or preventing access to certain markets or activities.

To address these problems, the Community needs to ensure credible enforcement of effective rules, applicable evenly to all, including to non-EC companies seeking short cuts to the profits generated by the integrated market. The Rome Treaty's provisions against public and private non-competitive behaviour will need to be applied in a manner consistent with the needs of the new market environment – and also to areas where its application is as yet in its early days.

A case in point is provided by the service sectors. As their deregulation gathers force, the advantages offered by the new dimension of the European home market become clearer. National markets appear less and less sufficient as a framework for exploiting the new competitive potential ushered in by liberalization. In sectors like telecommunications, air transport and financial services, the maximum play of EC-wide competition must be ensured, constrained only by issues of public interest like consumer and user safety, and the continued supply of essential services.

10 The global impact of the 1992 programme on the European economy – a macro-economic analysis of the gains from market integration

The supply-side shock: the macro-economic perspective
The Community's total gains from market integration, spelt out in chapter 9, can also be looked at through another, broader prism. From this wider angle, a more general picture emerges of the effects of the 1992 programme on the European economy's main indicators – on aggregates like gross domestic product, employment and inflation. To the micro-economic analysis of the preceding chapter is now added an outline of 1992's impact in a macro-economic perspective.

In one sense, by its sheer size, the supply-side shock administered by the White Paper programme is of macro-economic proportions. Although essentially aimed at business managers, the programme has undeniable implications for the managers of the general economy. It offers them a stronger basic economic performance and thus greater margins within which to conduct overall economic policy. Macro-economic strategy can be used as an amplifier to magnify the supply-side effects of the micro-economic manifesto set out in the White Paper.

Brief consideration of four examples serves to illustrate how growth in the EC is not just hampered directly by micro-economic constraints like non-tariff barriers, but also by macro-economic constraints operating at the level of the general economy:

i) *Public finances*: although now under better control, budget deficits continue by their size (still 4.4% of Gdp in 1987 after peaking at 5.5% in 1982) to put inordinate upward pressure on long-term interest rates, thereby penalizing productive investment, business activity, future growth and employment prospects.

ii) *The external constraint* : while for the EC as a whole the current trade balance has been positive since 1984 (1.1% of Gdp in 1987), deficits in some countries may constrain future growth. More important, the situation conceals a competitive warning :

in manufacturing, particularly high tech, European companies are steadily losing markets to Japan and the US. An underpriced dollar adds to this threat.

iii) *Inflation*, or the fear of its return despite the downward trend in the EC price index (13.4% in 1980, 7% in 1984, 3.2% in 1987), continues to dampen the outlook for economic growth.

iv) *Unemployment*: medium-term policies for sustainable economic growth are still inhibited by fears of their short-term impact on jobs, despite the stronger employment outlook they herald in the longer-run.

As the macro-economic analysis shows, all four of these major constraints on European growth will be significantly loosened by EC market integration, even if, in the case of employment, the gains – and considerable gains they are by any measure – will come in the medium term.

The methodology used in the analysis is described in detail elsewhere.[29] Suffice it to note here that it uses models which enable simulation of the main macro-economic mechanisms. These models enable not only the quantification of the macro-economic consequences of the 1992 programme but also the ways in which these effects will be channelled through the Community economy as a whole.

The analysis, whose results are summarised in the following pages (and in Table 10.1 on p.98), bases its quantification of these effects on an examination of four major aspects:[30]

• removal of customs barriers (section 1)
• opening up procurement markets (section 2)
• liberalisation of financial services (section 3)
• the supply-side effects: business strategies reacting to market integration and tougher competition (section 4).

Taken individually, each of these effects on the Community will tend to be magnified, or alternatively diminished, by the general workings of the EC economy – or by what might be called its macro-dynamic effects.[31] With this in mind, the chapter's final section looks at two general types of outcome: the macro-economic impact of market integration 'in the raw', ie. unassisted by economic policy; and second, the further potential for gains which would materialize if the additional leeway created by the removal of constraints were exploited by accompanying measures of general economic policy.

1 The removal of border controls
The removal of border controls will lead to downward pressures on

prices for intra-EC traded goods and services as a result of excess costs being eliminated (costs linked to border delays and red tape, see chapter 2 for details). Its macro-economic impact stems in large part from this price drop. Imports originating elsewhere in the EC will gain in competitivity in relation to items produced nationally or imported from outside the Community. This will lead to two corresponding types of substitution: intra-EC imports for national goods, intra-EC imports for extra-EC imports. There will be an improvement of each EC country's terms of trade as import prices drop (meaning that the same level of exports will buy more imports), and a positive impact on the trade balance of the Community as a whole. As a result, there could be an increase in EC Gdp of around 0.33% in the medium term.

By comparison to the initial savings from removing the direct costs of frontier formalities (see again Chapter 2), gains of the macro-dynamic type are likely to be limited. Indeed, job losses in customs-related areas and their knock-on effects might even lead to a slightly negative impact in the short-term, although this will be more than offset by significant improvements in the longer-run.

Abolition of customs barriers will have a favourable effect on public finances. On top of the short-term savings in expenditure on customs administration comes a medium-term rise in tax revenue, reflecting the boost to business activity given by frontier facilitation. The improvement in the balance of public finances should be around 0.2% of Gdp in the medium-term.

There will be a salutory impact on inflation. Any upward pressures on prices caused by greater economic activity will be far outweighed by the improvement in business costs and terms of trade noted above. A net deflationary effect of around 1% in price levels is expected for the medium term.

Yet, despite these quantified gains, the greatest impact is to be expressed qualitatively rather than in figures. For the integrated market to be credible, the barriers to be eliminated are psychological as well as economic. The removal of border formalities will provide the EC's economic actors with the symbolic certainty that the European home market is here to stay.

2 Opening up procurement markets

Liberalization of procurement markets, also strong in symbolic impact, will by and large have much greater measurable effect on the general economy than removal of customs barriers. Its macro-economic consequences will reverberate through the three main actors involved: public enterprises, public administrations and companies supplying public markets.

For public enterprises (providing eg. transport, energy, telecom services), procurement liberalization should mean big reductions in purchasing and investment costs, as capital goods in particular become cheaper under the competitive pressure of foreign suppliers (for examples, see Chapter 3). In a competitive environment, the downward push on their costs will in many sectors throughput to the prices they charge and this, in turn, will have a sizeable ripple effect in the rest of the economy. The main macro-economic impact will thus be two-fold – a downward pressure on the general price level and an upward push given to the EC's competitive position with the outside world.

Public administrations will reap two principal rewards – budget savings and larger tax revenues sparked by the thrust to business activity given by the newly-created competitive situation. With greater financial room for manoeuvre, governments should have three main options: reduce public debts, ease taxation, or directly boost demand. The first would by and large postpone the expected benefits, while either of the last two choices would mean direct support to growth and jobs.

For some traditional suppliers of public markets the story is different: they will need to reorganize and their cost structure will come under pressure. Moreover, there will be subsequent gains from these developments which will not be restricted to public markets. As a result, the beneficial effects will be felt on the market as a whole and thus serve to strengthen the macro-economic impacts described above.

Opening public procurement should, of itself and without accompanying measures of macro-economic support, mean an increase in Gdp of 0.5% and, in the process, provide nearly 400,000 new jobs in the medium-term. The growth prospect stems essentially from price reductions made by public enterprises and their knock-on effect on domestic and external demand.

In addition to the bonus for employment, growth in Gdp will be accompanied by improvement in all the other main indicators. The downward pressure on prices exerted by public enterprises should have a general deflationary impact of as much as 1.4% over the medium run. Gains in competitivity should lead to a slight strengthening of the Community's external position (+ 0.1% of Gdp). The medium-term gain for public finances would be more substantial (+ 0.3% of Gdp).

Once again, beyond the measured gains from EC public procurement liberalization lies another reality of immeasurable significance. This is that in opening up national markets, governments will be publicly nailing their colours to the mast of EC market integration, and thereby placing a vote of confidence in the supply side of the economy which business is likely to return in pursuit of its self-interest.

3 Liberalization of financial services

The economic effect of liberalizing these sectors – banking, insurance and securities services – is likely to be large even in its primary form. This is essentially due to the competitive shock administered to overpricing in the wake of market integration. But when scaled up to take full account of the role played by financial services in overall business activity, the overall macro-dynamic effect appears even more significant than outlined in Chapter 6.

Amplification of the basic effect will in large part be due to the lower cost of credit. Reduction in capital costs will encourage productive investment and thus sharply increase growth potential. Capital shortages, which could restrict the overall benefits from the integrated market, will be avoided. Liberalization of financial services, with the crucial supporting role they play right across the economy, should guarantee the wider availability of credit and better allocation of financial resources. A particular effect of general significance is the boost that cheaper credit should give to spending on housing, a sector known for its job-creating potential.

Beyond these gains, largely stemming from the lending activity of the banking sector, is the impact of the general lowering in the prices of financial services, in particular to industrial consumers whose costs thus diminish. The result will be to radiate a deflationary surge through the economy at large. This in turn will stimulate domestic demand by increasing purchasing power, and boost external demand by improving European competitivity. Households will benefit doubly. They will pay less for financial services and will gain from the general drop in prices.

Small wonder, then, that the overall macro-economic consequences of liberalising financial services are considerable. In the medium-term, the process should contribute an extra 1.5% to Community Gdp, its deflationary impact on price levels should be around 1.4%, and public finances should improve by an amount equal to around 1% of Gdp, mainly through a reduction in the debt burden. The EC's external balance would be subject to two conflicting forces: it would improve because of gains in European competitivity, but would suffer from the rise in imports, sucked in by higher investment and growth. As regards employment, lower financing costs might result in a degree of substitution of capital for labour, meaning short-term job losses, but the outlook created by new economic growth more than compensates for this. Medium-term estimates are for new jobs to increase by nearly half a million.

4. The supply-side effects: business strategies reacting to a new competitive environment

Putting a figure on the strategic response of the corporate sector to the new competitive environment bequeathed by EC market integration is a complex matter. Indeed, even with a clear view of the 1992 Community market, it is difficult to predict with accuracy the nature of business reactions to it, let alone quantify them as a macro-economic aggregate.

To tackle these problems, various illustrative scenarios were developed[32] – illustrative in the sense that they describe phenomena that are likely but not certain to occur. They seek to strike a balance between overstatement and understatement. They may make over-optimistic assumptions about the degree to which companies will convert market opportunities into economic success; on the other hand, they err by caution in not including all sectors and all effects in their aggregation. Thus the analysis looks at effects related to the direct costs of non-tariff barriers, to economies of scale, and at pure competition effects (lowering of monopoly profits, raising management efficiency). But it leaves to one side the impact of competition on investment and on innovation,[33] nor does it take account of transborder link-ups.

Two essential channels are taken by supply-side effects, which are intrinsically micro-economic, to project themselves onto the macro-economic stage:

– By reducing prices. Price reductions will develop in relation to the lowering of production costs. Competitive pressures will force companies into actively embarking on cost-cutting programmes through rationalization and improved economies of scale. Through inter-industry links, the lowering of upstream prices will reinforce reduction in downstream prices.
– By productivity gains in the factors of production, be they the result of more efficient allocation of resources (human, financial and technological), or industrial restructuring (economies of scale), or again improved internal business organization.

All the macro-economic consequences of the supply-side shock derive from these two factors, which in turn are conflicting in impact. Thus, the positive medium-term effects stemming from price reductions may be attenuated in the short-term by productivity gains. On the one hand, lower prices should stimulate domestic demand by real increases in income (particularly of households), and boost external demand by the gains they mean for European competitivity. But productivity gains imply cost savings in the factors of production – labour and capital – and these savings in turn have a depressant effect on demand.

From the interlocking dynamics of these two factors emerges a scenario of major medium-term gains to be won after initial challenges are met. Thus, in the short-term, productivity gains might mean a degree of job loss, but this dip in employment would be progressively filled and then spectacularly built on. The estimates for the medium-term are that the gains in the supply-side's efficiency and flexibility will lead to the creation of nearly a million new jobs. The short-term difficulties are inseparable from the longer-run benefits. To be eaten the cake has got to be baked.

If European business realises the potential gains on offer, the macro-economic effect should be very considerable. Supply-side success should mean the addition of 2% to Gdp in the medium-term, coupled with a substantial easing of the constraints on economic growth: a steep drop in prices (estimated at more than 2%), and improvements in public finances and in the EC's external position respectively equal to 0.6% and 0.4% of Gdp. A longer-term view would reveal a more favourable outcome as a result of a cumulative process.

5 Real and potential macro-economic gains from EC market integration

The overall picture is very positive. Whatever the effect analysed – removal of customs barriers, opening up public procurement, liberalization of financial services, or the supply-side effects – the macro-economic results appear consistently favourable for the Community in the medium-term.

Thus, according to our estimates (Table 10.1), EC market integration will in the medium-term:

- *trigger a major relaunch of economic activity*, adding on average 4.5% to EC Gdp;
- *simultaneously cool the economy*, deflating consumer prices by an average of 6.1%;
- *relax budgetary and external constraints*, improving the balance of public finances by an average equivalent to 2.2% of Gdp and boosting the EC's external position by around 1% of Gdp;
- *boost employment*, creating 1.8 million new jobs; although unable of itself to make big inroads into the present stock of unemployment, the effect would nonetheless be to reduce the jobless rate by around 1.5 percentage points.

The trigger-point: removal of market barriers

The trigger-point for all these gains (graphically presented in the flow-chart below) should not be forgotten. It is the removal of non-tariff barriers. This is synonymous with the reduction in production costs which, under the pressure of strengthened competition, exerts downward pressure on prices. From this starting point come:

- purchasing power gains, which stimulate economic activity;
- competitivity gains which, in addition to providing another growth stimulant, improve the external balance;
- the initial lowering of prices, not just inhibiting demand-push inflation, but actually leading to deflation;
- the easing of public deficits, under the dual impact of open public procurement and economic regeneration.

Beyond this, in the longer-term, further gains are in prospect as the 'virtuous circle' effect (see also Chapter 9, section 4) once again takes hold. Under the pressure of competition and the continental broadening of the home market, companies will be engaged in a

Table 10.1 Macroeconomic consequences of EC market integration for the Community in the medium term

	Customs formal-ities	Public procure-ment	Financial services	Supply-side effects[1]	Average value	Total Spread
Relative changes (%)						
Gdp	0.4	0.5	1.5	2.1	4.5	(3.2 – 5.7)
Consumer prices	–1.0	–1.4	–1.4	–2.3	–6.1	(–4.5 – –7.7)
Absolute changes						
Employment						
(millions)	200	350	400	850	1800	(1300 – 2300)
Budgetary balance						
(% point of Gdp)	0.2	0.3	1.1	0.6	2.2	(1.5 – 3.0)
External balance						
(% point of Gdp)	0.2	0.1	0.3	0.4	1.0	(0.7 – 1.3)

Source: HERMES (EC Commission and national teams) and INTERLINK (OECD) economic models[2]

Notes:
1 Based on a scenario which includes the supply-side effects estimated by the consultants, economies of scale in manufacturing industry and competition effects (monopoly rent, X-inefficiency).
2 The INTERLINK simulations have been carried out by the Commission departments. The OECD takes no responsibility for the use of the model.

permanent search for lower costs. The beneficial effects stemming from the reduction in production costs and productivity gains thus become a self-sustaining process.

All these gains, it should be emphasized, would be achieved in a situation where macro-economic policy remained unchanged. They thus represent the raw, unaccompanied benefits to the Community economy of EC market integration, expressed in macro-economic terms.

Economic outlook and the policy variable

This prospect of relaxing the major economic constraints – inflation, unemployment, public and trade deficits – in turn opens up a further and durable potential for growth in the medium and longer term: ie. beyond the raw benefits.

Take, for example, the easing of pressure on public deficits. This may lead governments to consider policies of accelerated repayments of public debts, in which case the return to balanced budgets would also be accelerated. But even in a scenario of stringent orthodoxy, where first priority is given to balancing the public books, greater room would become available in the longer run for consideration of more expansionist policy options. The relaxing of economic constraints might also lead to shorter term action of this type, eg. lowering taxes or participation in major European infrastructure projects. In this case, untying the budgetary constraint would clearly have an immediate and positive impact on the level of economic activity. Similarly, any improvement in the external balance or drop in the inflation rate means, sooner or later, an injection of economic growth.

Clearly, given the size of budget deficits in the EC, the positive impact of market integration on public finances (estimated at 2.2% of Gdp) will play a key role in whatever economic policy is chosen. The main effects of three distinct policy scenarios are outlined in Table 10.2. Each of them, to a greater or lesser extent, uses the budgetary surplus generated by the 1992 programme.

The full conversion of the budgetary gain into economic growth (scenario 1) is mentioned here purely for illustrative purposes because its implementation, although leading to a medium-term rise in Gdp of 7.5% and in employment of almost 6 million, would lead to a significant deterioration of the external balance by an amount equal to 0.5% of Gdp. In the second policy scenario, possibly erring on the side of caution, the external constraint is fully removed and, using only part of the budgetary gains, there still results an increase in Gdp of almost 6.5% and job creation of the order of 4 million.

The third scenario, situated half-way between the first two, may

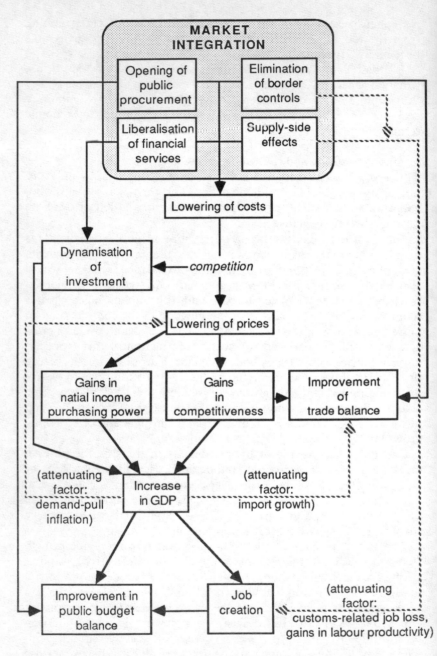

Chart 10.1 Principal macroeconomic mechanisms activated in the course of
completing the internal market

100

Table 10.2 Macro-economic consequences of EC market integration accompanied by economic policy measures (medium-term)

Name of economic policy	Margin for manoeuvre exploited	Economic consequences				
		Gdp (in%)	Consumer prices (in%)	Employment (in millions)	Public budget balance (in% point Gdp)	External balance (in% point Gdp)
Without accompanying measures (see Table 10.1)		4.5	-6.1	1.8	2.2	1.0
With accompanying measures[1]	– Public budget balance	7.5	-4.3	5.7	0	-0.5
	– External balance	6.5	-4.9	4.4	0.7	0
	– Price reductions[2]	7.0	-4.5	5.0	0.4	-0.2
Margin of accuracy				± 30%		

Source: HERMES (EC Commission and national teams) and INTERLINK (OECD) economic models[3]

Notes:

1 Accompanying economic policy measures (increased public investment, income tax reductions) are calibrated so that all the room for manoeuvre created by market integration for alternatively public balances, external balances and price reductions is fully used.

2 In this case, accompanying economic policy was calibrated so as to use 25% of the deflationary reservoir created by consumer price reductions. Full use of the margin for manoeuvre created by price reductions could have led to a totally unrealistic outcome (including, in particular, massive deterioration in the EC's external position).

3 The INTERLINK simulations have been carried out by the Commission departments. The OECD takes no responsibility for the use of the model.

be considered the most plausible. It involves partial exploitation of the margins of manoeuvre created by both price deflation and budgetary gains, but makes slightly more than full use of the EC's external balance. This mid-way economic policy response to European market integration leads to striking results. There would be a medium-term increase in Gdp of 7%, unaccompanied by inflation, and the creation of 5 million new jobs. And it would still leave governments with a hefty budgetary gain from market integration (equal to 0.7% of Gdp) on which to cushion their concern for financial orthodoxy.

11 Getting the most out of the European home market – guidelines for maximum success

The potential inherent in the 1992 programme for providing the Community and its member states with major economic gains has been outlined in the preceding pages. Whether expressed in terms of economic welfare (Chapter 9) or leading macro-economic indicators like growth, employment and inflation (Chapter 10), this message emerges with unequivocal clarity.

Whatever their different starting points, and even granting a fairly broad margin of error, the micro-economic and macro-economic estimates converge on medium-term gains of around 4%-7% of EC gross domestic product. Among the various indicators of this success, the most crucial is without doubt employment. While recent years have often been marked by lengthy debates about demand-led growth, our analysis shows that the improvements to the supply-side of the economy set out in the Community's 1992 manifesto is the *sine qua non* for a stronger European labour market outlook.[34] Supply-side policies will favour job creation precisely because their effect is to reduce costs and prices. These reductions will lead to growth in demand, growth in output, and thus growth in employment. Moreover, strengthening the supply-side's flexibility and competitivity – in other words, strengthening European business – will additionally magnify the beneficial impact of policies seeking economic growth through stimulating demand.

That said, the precise time-frame for realizing in full the beneficial effects of the main measures set out in the 1992 White Paper is difficult to establish. Moreover, it differs depending on the measure considered. Thus the impact of removing the delays caused by border formalities is short-term, while the impulse given by market integration to, for example, industrial restructuring and innovation will result in longer term benefits. Similarly, while significant job creation is expected in the medium-term, there are risks of short-term losses.

Getting an accurate handle on the time-frame for these gains is complicated by a further factor. This is the uncertainty linked to the dynamics which produce the two main types of beneficial effect from market integration. The first type of effect is a once-and-for-all shock leading to Gdp growth, a good example of which is again the removal of intra-EC customs formalities. But the second type is less easy to pin down. Examples of this include product and process innovation which will modify – upwards – the entire trajectory of EC growth and economic welfare throughout the 1990s and beyond into the twenty-first century.

The challenge – political and social, not just economic
The speed with which the gains are realized will of course be influenced by the costs of adjusting to the market environment in which the benefits can be fully reaped. These adjustments, clearly a substantial challenge for the authors of the 1992 programme, take various forms. Changes in price rigidities, in the productivity of factors of production (labour, capital), in the economic policies of EC member governments – these are so many potential threats to protected positions, be they those of companies, industries, regions or nations. Restructuring entire sectors, shifts in employment, new demands on labour mobility and training, the regional distribution of new wealth – these are so many factors whose adjustment to the new market conditions carries their own social and political costs. The road to market integration, however paved with good intentions, leads to 1992 by way of hard decisions rather than easy options.

Guidelines for success
Realizing the full economic potential of the 1992 programme means changes in the behaviour of the European economy's main actors and the pursuance of appropriate policies by EC governments.

Business If EC market integration is to succeed, so must business. The degree of its success depends on the strategic response of Europe's companies to the market challenge, and on their ability to seize the new opportunities on offer (see Chapter 9). Other challenges facing corporate management are how to help make industrial relations less conflictual, encourage employee involvement in the life of the company, and ensure that workers share in the productivity gains jointly achieved with management. Most important, business must keep the pressure on governments to live up to their 1992 commitments.

Competition policy If home market conditions are to be maintained, so must a firm and credible European competition policy. Without it, there can be no guarantee that lower production costs will be passed on in the form of lower prices. And without that, the

104

stimulus given to demand by the supply-side, taking the dual form of higher domestic purchasing power and greater external competitivity, will be still-born. Beyond this, rigorous maintenance of the Community's competititive processes is the central regulator of the market's machinery for technology innovation, product quality and good management.

Wealth redistribution If the new rewards are not shared fairly, the EC home market will rest on a brittle skein of regional and social tensions. There are strong arguments for measures to attenuate the negative impact of market integration on wealth distribution, and to ensure that differences in economic performance between EC countries are not intensified. At the same time, it should not be taken for granted that the impact will be inordinately negative, prefiguring an outlook of unbridled economic Darwinism. Indeed, recent developments in trade theory[35] and past experience, eg. with the removal of intra-EC tariff barriers, indicate that redistributive effects in the wake of freer trade need not be excessive. Undoubtedly, however, assistance will be needed for the Community's declining regions and labour affected by industrial restructuring.

At the same time, the potential gains from market integration should help reinforce the consensus around the 1992 programme which European employers and labour began to forge in 1985. The new prospect of dynamic growth rates leading to major medium-term job creation should also assist the process. Beyond this, however, as indicated in a recent Commission report[36] there is a need to examine the sector-by-sector impact of removing non-tariff barriers, and to envisage accompanying social policy measures across a range of fields: vocational training and mobility; labour market flexibility; and more intensive use of the Community's social and regional funds. The extent to which the 1992 programme can attract economic and social cohesion around it will be key to its chances of success. It will be built neither on a centralized Community strategy nor disparate national practice, but on a flexible approach anchored in a common core of minimum social arrangements.

General economic policy If the full potential of the EC internal market is to be realized, non-inflationary policies of macro-economic growth, convergently pursued, seem ineluctable. As shown in Chapter 10, such policies could be undertaken on a largely risk-free basis, whether the governmental priority is set on public finances, consumer prices, employment or the external position. But, in the 1992 home market, it is impossible to conceive how such policies can be pursued other than on a convergent basis. Otherwise, the home

105

market will cease very rapidly to be a home market. Its completion means a very high level of economic interdependence – free trade in goods, services, people and capital between its constituent countries. This interdependence cannot be sustained in a macro-economic policy void.

In the past, there has been no shortage of examples of how deflationary spirals can be triggered between closely interdependent countries pursuing divergent economic policies. Experience also shows how countries, linked in such close relationships, often choose to resolve policy divergences or trade imbalances by recessionary rather than expansionist measures. The well-known beggar-thy-neighbour reflex passes on part of the buck to trading partners, in the shape of losses in competitivity and contracting export markets. By contrast, the growth option leads to a spread of new wealth. The first policy leads to an export of costs, the second to an export of benefits.

To avoid the deflationary threat, strengthening the coordination between EC member states' economic policies is a commonsense imperative. Also, a European home market is likely to increase exchange rate fluctuations: intensification of intra-EC trade and liberalisation of trans-border capital movements – indispensable as they are for achieving the gains of market integration – may well heighten monetary instability. Success in creating the internal market thus condemns the Community to strengthen the European monetary system and build the institutional framework needed to guarantee intra-EC exchange rate stability.

Governments If they fail to give credibility to the 1992 programme, it is hard to see how or why business should respond and realise its potential gains. Companies will not launch themselves into major strategic choices without evidence of the political commitment on which they are in part based.

The White Paper programme, a sort of political guarantee of European commercial risk, requires rapid enactment. More than this, governments need to show that the legislation it contains is irreversible once enacted. The law's delays, muddled decision-making, obscure compromises – failure, in short, to seize the political opportunity today – will be repaid in kind by the missed market opportunity of tomorrow. What is Europe's greatest opportunity is within its collective grasp. In seizing it Europeans will not only do themselves justice now, but bequeath a legacy of durable wealth and stability to future generations.

Notes

Summary and conclusions

1   Ecu at 1985 value, the year of most of the statistical evidence used in the research. The centrepoint of the estimated spread of Ecu 174 – 258 billion is Ecu 216 billion.
    As at mid-March 1988 the exchange rate of the Ecu was as follows:
    1 Ecu = 0.671 £ sterling
          = 0.775 Irish punt
          = 1.217 US$
2   Commission of the EC, *White Paper on Completing the Internal Market*, Brussels, 1985.
3   See also Commission of the EC, *Efficiency, Stability and Equity – A Strategy for the Evolution of the Economic System of the European Community*, Report of a study group appointed by the EC Commission and presided by T. Padoa-Schioppa, Brussels, 1987; Commission des CE, *La dimension sociale du marché intérieur*, rapport d'étape du Groupe interservices présidé par M. J. Degimbe, Brussels, 1988.

Chapter 1
4   Commission of the EC, *White Paper on Completing the Internal Market*, op. cit.

Chapter 2

5   Commission of the EC, *Research on the 'Cost of Non-Europe' – The Completion of the Internal Market: a survey of European industry's perception of the likely effects*, by G. Nerb, Brussels, (forthcoming).
6   Commission of the EC, *The Economics of 1992 – An Assessment of the Potential Economic Effects of Completing the Internal Market of the EC*, Brussels, (Part C, p.3.2.3), March 1988.
7   According to information from the Association Européenne de Vente par Correspondance, Brussels, February 1986.

Chapter 3

8   Calculations based on Independent European Programme Group (I.E.P.G.) Report, report of a group of independent experts presided by H. Vredeling, NATO, Brussels, 1987.

Chapter 4
9   Commission of the EC, *Research on the 'Cost of Non-Europe' – The Completion of the Internal Market: a survey of European industry's perception of the likely effects*, op. cit.
10   ibid.

11 Speech by European Commissioner K. H. Narjes to the Council of Ministers, 1983.

12 'Cassis de Dijon' Judgment by the European Court of Justice, CJEC 20.2.1979 (Rewe-Zentral AG v Bundesmonopolverwaltung für Branntwein), 120/78:(1979) ECR 649.

Chapter 6

13 For the part played by the financial services sector in calculating the overall gains to the European economy from the elimination of market-related costs, see Chapter 9.

14 *France Telecom*, no. 63, October 1987, p. 47.

Chapter 7

15 These figures are to be interpreted with caution, because prices may reflect quality differences. Furthermore, R&D costs are sometimes paid out of a different budget and thus not reflected in the competitive world market prices. Thus, a complete move of European equipment prices to the competitive world market levels indicated might not sustain the amount of R&D necessary. Viable *long term* competitive price levels are more likely to be 20% above the world prices indicated.

Chapter 8

16 For full treatment of the micro-economic analysis, see Commission of the EC, *The Economics of 1992 – An Assessment of the Potential Economic Effects of Completing the Internal Market of the EC*, op.cit.

Chapter 9

17 Boston Consulting Group, *Les mécanismes fondamentaux de la compétitivité*, Hommes et Techniques, 1981.

18 For a full analysis see Commission of the EC, *The Economics of 1992 – An Assessment of the Potential Economic Effects of Completing the Internal Market of the EC*, op.cit.

19 A more restrictive hypothesis for high barrier sectors is that the level of price peaks are only reduced by half of the gap separating them from the average of the two lowest prices. In this latter case, savings are estimated at around 2.8% of Gdp.

20 Commission of the EC, *Research on the 'Cost of Non-Europe' – An Assessment based on a Formal Model of Imperfect Competition and Economies of Scale*, by Smith, A., Venables, A., Brussels, (forthcoming).

21 Scherer, F.M., *Industrial Market Structure and Economic Performance*, second edn, Houghton Mifflin.

22 Commission of the EC, *Research on the 'Cost of Non-Europe' – Competition and Innovation*, study carried out for the Commission of the EC by Geroski, P.A., Brussels, (forthcoming); and Kamien, M.I., and Schwartz, N.L., *Market Structure and Innovations*, Cambridge University Press, 1982

23 Commission of the EC, *The Completion of the Internal Market: a survey of European industry's perception of the likely effects*, op. cit.

24 Commission of the EC, *16th Report on Competition Policy*, Brussels, 1987, Part Four.

25 For further examples see de Woot, Ph., 'Capacité stratégique et performance économique à long terme des entreprises européennes dans les secteurs à haute technologie', Projet Pénélope for the Commission of the EC, *FAST – Occasional Papers*, Brussels, 1987.

26 Commission of the EC, *16th Report on Competition Policy*, op.cit.

27 See Commission of the EC, *Research on the 'Cost of Non-Europe' – Obstacles to Transborder Business Activity*, Study carried out for the Commission of the EC by European Research Associates & Prognos, Brussels, (forthcoming).

28 Jacquemin, A., *The New Industrial Organisation*, MIT and Oxford University Press, 1987

Chapter 10

29 For a detailed description of the two models HERMES (EC Commission and national teams) and INTERLINK (OECD) see Commission of the EC, *The Economics of 1992 – An Assessment of the Potential Economic Effects of Completing the Internal Market of the EC*, op.cit.

30 See Catinat, M., 'Radioscopie du grand marché intérieur', *Economie Prospective Internationale*, 1988, No. 33, CEPII, 1er trimestre, Documentation française.

31 ibid.

32 See Commission of the EC, *The Economics of 1992 – An Assessment of the Potential Economic Effects of Completing the Internal Market of the EC*, op.cit.

33 See Geroski, P.A., Jacquemin, A., 'Corporate Competitiveness in Europe', *Economic Policy*, No. 1, November, 1985, pp. 170-217; and Jacquemin, A., *The New Industrial Organisation*, op. cit.

Chapter 11

34 For further details see Chapter 10, in particular Table 10.2.

35 Helpman, E., and Krugman., P., *Market Structure and Foreign Trade: increasing returns, imperfect competition and the international economy*, MIT Press, 1985.

36 For further details see Commission des CE, *La dimension sociale du marché intérieur*, rapport d'étape du Groupe interservices présidé par M. J. Degimbe, op.cit.

Bibliography

Albert, M., et Ball, R.J., 'Vers le redressement de l'économie
européenne dans les années 80', *Rapport présenté au Parlement
européen*.

Boston Consulting Group, *Les mécanismes fondamentaux de la
compétitivité*, Hommes et Techniques, 1981.

Catinat, M., 'Radioscopie du grand marché intérieur', *Economie
Prospective Internationale*, 1988, No. 33, CEPII, 1er trimestre,
Documentation française.

Commission of the European Communities, 'The single act: a new
frontier for Europe', *Bulletin of the European Communities*, 1987,
supplement 1/87.

Commission of the EC, *Efficiency, Stability and Equity – A Strategy
for the Evoluton of the Economic System of the European Community*,
Report of a study group appointed by the EC Commission and
presided by T. Padoa-Schioppa, Brussels, 1987.

Commission of the EC, *16th Report on Competition Policy*, Brussels,
1987.

Commission of the EC, *The Economics of 1992 – An Assessment of the
Potential Economic Effects of Completing the Internal Market of the
EC*, Brussels, (forthcoming).

Commission of the EC, *White Paper on Completing the Internal
Market*, Brussels, 1985.

de Woot, Ph., 'Capacité stratégique et performance économique à
long terme des entreprises européennes dans les secteurs à haute
technologie', *Projet Pénélope*, Brussels, 1987.

Helpman, E., and Krugman, P., *Market Structure and Foreign Trade:
increasing returns, imperfect competition and the international economy*,
MIT Press, 1985.

Jacquemin, A., *The New Industrial Organisation*, MIT and Oxford
University Press, 1987.

Kamien, M.I., and Schwartz, N.L., *Market Structure and Innovations*,
Cambridge University Press.

Motor Industry Research Unit, *A Study into the Economic Implications
of a European Internal Market from the Perspective of the Volume
Automotive Sector*, A Report commissioned by Ford of Europe for
the EC Commission, Brussels, 1988.

Owen, N., *Economies of Scale, Competitiveness and Trade Patterns*

110

within the European Community, Clarendon Press, Oxford, 1983.

Pelkmans, J., *Market Integration in the European Community*, Martinus Nijhoff Publishers, 1984.

Scherer, F.M., *Industrial Market Structure and Economic Performance*, second edn, Houghton Mifflin.

Vignon, J., 'Sept ans pour construire le vrai marché commun', *Economie Prospective Internationale*, 1986, No. 25, CEPII, 1er trimestre, Documentation française.

APPENDICES
PRESENTATION OF
THE 'RESEARCH ON
THE COST OF
NON-EUROPE'

Appendix 1   The structure of the research

The purpose of the research was to provide a solid body of scientific analysis regarding the costs of European market fragmentation, and thus the benefits on offer following the removal of barriers targetted by the Commission's *White Paper on Completing the Internal Market*, which was adopted by the European Community summit in 1985.

A preliminary to embarking on the research was the establishment of a steering committee, bringing together the multi-faceted expertise needed to effectively oversee the project and the reports undertaken for it by independent consultants. As its name suggests, the committee helped to steer a course through the uncharted seas of inexistent basic data and methodologies. Its combination of Commission civil servants, mainly drawn from the two most directly concerned departments (directorates-general II and III), and leading outside experts proved to be a determining asset in the success of the operation.

At the outset, the committee opted to make two key choices:

– to limit the scope of the 'non-Europe' research to the market and trade barriers to be eliminated by the White Paper programme;
– to ensure that the coverage of the individual studies, which were to be launched in the course of the project, included the four major Community countries, while leaving open the possibility of extending this geographical scope on a case by case basis.

In carrying out the research, whose structure and main participants are outlined below, these two choices have been applied with due flexibility. In particular, the need to achieve as broad a geographical coverage as possible has been satisfied both in many of the individual studies and in the industrial survey in which 11,000 enterprises across the Community actively participated; and, perhaps more significantly still, by the aggregate economic estimates to be found in Part II. In addition, to ensure maximum coherence in the methodological approach adopted by the project and in the presentation of its results, two symposia were held between the Commission and the independent consultants in respectively May and October 1987.

Since the outset of the research, the steering committee gave special emphasis to the need to develop analytic tools which would enable identification and quantitative evaluation of the dynamic effects generated by the elimination of non-tariff barriers – effects which, it was strongly felt, would provide the most significant contribution to the resultant welfare benefits. These tools were developed in the early months of the research, when the first sketch of what was to become the methodology used in the macro-economic analysis was outlined.The same effort was made for the micro-economic analysis, starting with a round table of leading economists on economies of scale.

This book represents the most visible part of the results of the research project. In the interests of wider circulation, it does not treat in detail the methodology used to obtain the results, nor does it report all the findings of the basic studies carried out by the consultants. Appendix II supplies the list of publications in which the detailed results of the research can be found.

Criticism is expected and welcome. Such an enterprise cannot be immune to imperfection and even perhaps error. However the overall outcome of the research, which points to very significant gains to be derived from European market integration, seem to be both accurate and reasonable. It is highly unlikely that the intellectual input of so many leading consultants, academics, officials and independent experts would be unanimously pointing in the wrong direction.

Director
Paolo CECCHINI   Special Advisor to the Commission
                                  of the European Communities

Coordinator
Michael LOY   Commission of the European
                                  Communities

Steering Committee

Chairman:
Paolo CECCHINI

External members:
Sergio ALESSANDRINI   Università Bocconi, Milano
Paul CHAMPSAUR   Ministère de l'Economie, des
                                  Finances et du Budget, Paris

116

Jean-Michel CHARPIN	Centre d'Etudes Prospectives et d'Informations Internationales, Paris
Michel DELEAU	European Investment Bank, Luxembourg
Wolfgang GERSTENBERGER	IFO–Institut für Wirtschaftsforschung, München
Peter HOLMES	University of Sussex, Brighton
Alexis JACQUEMIN	Université de Louvain-La-Neuve
Jacques PELKMANS	European Institute of Public Administration, Maastricht
Carlo SECCHI	Università Bocconi, Milano
Manfred WEGNER	IFO-Institut für Wirtschaftsforschung, München

Commission of the European Communities:

Michel AUJEAN	Directorate-General Economic and Financial Affairs
Michel AYRAL	Directorate-General Internal Market and Industrial Affairs
Michel CATINAT	Directorate-General Economic and Financial Affairs
Michel EMERSON	Directorate-General Economic and Financial Affairs
Philippe GOYBET	Directorate-General Economic and Financial Affairs
Michael LOY	Directorate-General Internal Market and Industrial Affairs
Jean-François MARCHIPONT	Directore-General Internal Market and Industrial Affairs

Former members:

Willi LEIBFRITZ	IFO-Institut für Wirtschaftsforschung, München
Geoffrey SHEPHERD	University of Sussex, Brighton
Giovanni RAVASIO	Directorate-General Economic and Financial Affairs
Jacques SOENENS	Directorate-General Internal Market and Industrial Affairs

Economic Analysis Team

Michael EMERSON	Directorate-General Economic and Financial Affairs
Michel AUJEAN	Directorate-General Economic and Financial Affairs

Richard CAWLEY	Directorate-General Economic and Financial Affairs
Fabienne ILZKOVITZ	Directorate-General Economic and Financial Affairs
Marc VANHEUKELEN	Directorate-General Economic and Financial Affairs
Marianne KLINGBEIL	Directorate-General Economic and Financial Affairs
Morten JUNG-OLSEN	Directorate-General Economic and Financial Affairs
Philippe GOYBET	Directorate-General Economic and Financial Affairs
Michael GREEN	Directorate-General Economic and Financial Affairs
Angelo REATI	Directorate-General Economic and Financial Affairs
Brendan CARDIFF	Directorate-General Economic and Financial Affairs
Pierre BUIGUES	Directorate-General Economic and Financial Affairs
Silvano PRESA	Directorate-General Economic and Financial Affairs
Michel CATINAT[1,2]	Directorate-General Economic and Financial Affairs
Alexander ITALIANER[2]	Directorate-General Economic and Financial Affairs
Pierre VALETTE[2]	Directorate-General Science, Research and Development
Eric DONNI[2]	Directorate-General Science, Research and Development
Gernot NERB[3]	Directorate-General Economic and Financial Affairs
Christopher SMYTH[3]	Directorate-General Economic and Financial Affairs

1 methodology
2 econometric modelling
3 industrial business survey

Coordinating Team
Michael LOY
Maria BRINDLMAYER   Consultante, Brussels
Andrea FORTI   Consultant, Milano

Administrative Coordination
Ursula NIEBERDING   Directorate-General Internal
                          Market and Industrial Affairs

Book
John ROBINSON   European Research Associates,
                          Brussels

Studies and Consultancies

Basic Information	Consultant	Supervision	DG
The 'Cost of Non-Europe' in Public Sector Procurement	WS ATKINS MANAGEMENT CONSULTANTS, Epsom/Surrey	Philippe GOYBET	II.B.3
		Pierre BUIGUES	II.B.3
		Fabienne ILZKOVITZ	II.B.1
		Robert COLEMAN	III.F
		Reginald SPENCE	III.A–Co
		David WHITE	III.F.1
		Gerhard LOHAN	III.F.1
		George W. O'BRIEN	III.F.1
		Peter HOLMES	
The 'Cost of Non-Europe': Customs Barriers	ERNST & WHINNEY Management Consultants, London	Michel AUJEAN	II.B.1
		Pierre BUIGUES	II.B.3
		Morten JUNG-OLSEN	II.B.1
		Michel AYRAL	III.A.2
		Jean-Arnold VINOIS	III.A.3
		Gaspard FRONTINI	VII–PCU
		Dominique PAVARD	VII–PCU
		Christian BOURGIN	XIX.B
The 'Cost of Non-Europe': An illustration in the Road Haulage Sector		Raoul PRADO	XXI.B.3
		Nikolaus VAULONT	XXI.C.2
		Max KRAEMER	XXI.B.1
		Pierre FAUCHERAND	XXI.B.1
		Geralyn DONALDSON	XXI.C.2
		Graham SIMS	
		Paul CHAMPSAUR	
The 'Cost of Non-Europe': Obstacles to transborder business activity	EUROPEAN RESEARCH ASSOCIATES, Bruxelles/ PROGNOS, Basel	Richard CAWLEY	II.B.1
		Michel AYRAL	III.A.2
		Jean-Arnold VINOIS	III.A.2
		Karl GLEICHMANN	XV.B.3
		Carlo SECCHI	
The 'Cost of Non-Europe': Technical Barriers in six Industries	GROUPE MAC, Paris	Marc VANHEUKELEN	II.B.1
		Thomas GARVEY	III.B
		Ernesto PREVIDI	III.B.1
		Wolfgang GERSTENBERGER	
Removal of Technical Trade Barriers	GEWIPLAN GMBH Gesellschaft für Wirtschaftsför-derung und Marktplanung, Frankfurt	Marc VANHEUKELEN	II.B.1
		Karlheinz ZACHMANN	III.B.3
		Jean-Charles JANSEN	III.B.3
		Pablo AYALA FERNANDEZ	III.B.3
		Wolfgang GERSTENBERGER	
The 'Cost of Non-Europe' in Financial Services	PRICE WATERHOUSE, London	Michael GREEN	II.B.3
		Richard CAWLEY	II.B.1
		Peter SMITH	III.A.4
		Olivier RUYSSEN	III.A.4
		Jean-Pierre DE LAET	IV.A.3
		Peter TROBERG	XV.A.4
		Will. HARRIS-BURLAND	XV.A.4
		Volker HEYDT	XV.A.4
		Manfred WEGNER	

Basic Information	Consultant	Supervision	DG
The 'Cost of Non-Europe' for Business Services	PEAT, MARWICK & McLINTOCK, London	Michael GREEN Vict. POU-SERRADELL Peter SMITH Olivier RUYSSEN Carlo SECCHI	II.B.3 III.A.4 III.A.4 III.A.4
The Benefits of Completing the Internal Market for Telecommunication – Services and – Equipment in the Community	INSEAD – Institut Européen d'Administration des Affaires, Fontainebleau	Brendan CARDIFF Marianne KLINGBEIL Christian GARRIC Joel LE QUEMENT Alison BIRKETT Peter HOLMES	II.B.3 II.B.1 XIII.D.1 XIII.E.3 XIII–Exp.
The 'Cost of Non-Europe' in the Foodstuff industry	GROUPE MAC, Paris	Pierre BUIGUES Dorian PRINCE Gwenole COZIGOU Jacques PELKMANS	II.B.3 III.B.2 III.B.2
The EC92 Automobile Sector	LUDVIGSEN ASSOCIATES LIMITED, London	Angelo REATI Marianne KLINGBEIL Daniele VERDIANI Roger PEETERS Dorian PRINCE Paul VIGIER Jean-Michel CHARPIN	II.B.3 II.B.1 III.C. III.C.1 III.B.2 III.C.1
The 'Cost of Non-Europe' in the Pharmaceutical Industry	EAG – Economists Advisory Group, London	Angelo REATI Fernand SAUER Jacques PELKMANS	II.B.3 III.B.6
Le Coût de la Non-Europe dans le domaine des produits de construction	BIPE – Bureau d'Information et de Prévisions Economiques, Neuilly-sur-Seine	Silvano PRESA William TULLY Raymond MOURAREAU Michel DELEAU	II.B.3 III.B.5 III.B.5
The 'Cost of Non-Europe' in the Textile-Clothing Industry	IFO – Institut für Wirtschaftsforschung, München/ PROMETEIA CALCOLO, Bologna	Michel AUJEAN Silvano PRESA Daniele VERDIANI Paul RUTSAERT Heinz BERZAU Sergio ALESSANDRINI	II.B.1 II.B.3 III.C III.C.2 III.C.2

Industrial Survey	Consultant	Supervision	DG
The Completion of the Internal Market	Banque Nationale de Belgique, Bruxelles Denmarks Statistik, Kobenhavn IFO – Institut für Wirtschaftsforschung, München	Gernot NERB Christopher SMYTH	II–C.Ec. II.1.CIS

121

Industrial Survey	*Consultant*	*Supervision*	*DG*
A survey of European Industry's perception of the likely effects	IEIR – Institute for Economic Research, Athens Ministerio de Industria y Energia, Madrid INSEE – Institut National de la Statistique et des Etudes Economiques, Paris CII – Confederation of Irish Industry, and ESRI – Economic and Social Research Institute, Dublin ISCO – Istituto Nazionale per lo studio della congiuntura, Roma IRB – Independent Research Bureau Europe SPRL, Bruxelles/ Luxembourg NIPO – Het Nederlands Instituut voor de Publieke Opinie en het Marketonderzoek BV, Amsterdam INE – Instituto Nacional de Estatistica, Lisboa Confederation of British Industry, London		

Economic Analysis	*Consultant*	*Supervision*	*DG*
Bibliography on Barriers within the US Internal Market	Benedict WELSH, Washington	Marc VANHEUKELEN	II.B.1

Economic Analysis	Consultant	Supervision	DG
The Internal Markets of North America – fragmentation and integration in the US and Canada	Jacques PELKMANS, Maastricht in cooperation with	Marc VANHEUKELEN	
Commerce Intra-Branche: Performances des firmes et analyse des échanges commerciaux dans la Communauté européenne	C.I.R.E.M. – Club d'Information et de Reflexion sur l'Economie Mondiale, Paris	Michel AUJEAN Jean-François MARCHIPONT Sergio ALESSANDRINI	II.B.1 III.A.3
A Survey of the Economies of Scale	Cliff PRATTEN, Department of Applied Economics, University of Cambridge	Michel AUJEAN Fabienne ILZKOVITZ Pierre BUIGUES Alexis JACQUEMIN	II.B.1 II.B.1 II.B.3
Economies of Scale and Intra-Community Trade	Joachim SCHWALBACH, International Institute of Management, Berlin	Alexis JACQUEMIN	
Competition and Innovation	Paul GEROSKI, London Business School	Alexis JACQUEMIN	
The Costs of Non-Europe: An Assessment based on a Formal Model of Imperfect Competition and Economies of Scale	Alasdair SMITH/Anthony VENABLES, University of Sussex	Alexis JACQUEMIN	
Economies of Scale and European Integration: the Case of Italy	Rodolfo HELG, Pippo RANCI, Istituto per la Ricerca Sociale – IRS, Milano	Alexis JACQUEMIN	
Partial Equilibrium Calculation of the Impact of Internal Market Barriers in the European Community	Michael DAVENPORT, London in cooperation with	Alexis JACQUEMIN Richard CAWLEY	II.B.1

123

Economic Analysis	Consultant	Supervision	DG
Actualisation partielle de modèles macro-économiques. Préparation de simulations permettant l'évaluation de l'impact de l'achèvement du marché intérieur	ESTARTE, Bruxelles	Michel CATINAT Alexander ITALIANER Pierre VALETTE Eric DONNI	II–C.Ec. II.C.4 XII.E.5 XII.E.5
Utilisation du modèle HERMES Belgique, Royaume-Uni, Italie, France, à l'analyse macroéconomique et sectorielle de l'achèvement du marché intérieur	ESAP, Bruxelles CAMBRIDGE ECONO-METRICS, Cambridge PROMETEIA, Bologna EURECO, Vanves	Michel CATINAT Alexander ITALIANER Pierre VALETTE Eric DONNI	II.–C.Ec. II.C.4 XII.E.5 XII.E.5
Conséquences macroéconomiques de l'achèvement du marché intérieur – l'enseignement des modèles		Michel CATINAT Alexander ITALIANER Eric DONNI	II–C.Ec. II.C.4 XII.E.5

124

Appendix II *The publication programme*

Publications by the Office for Official Publications of the European Communities, Luxembourg

The economics of 1992: an assessment of the potential economic effects of completing the internal market of the European Community.

EUROPEAN ECONOMY, no. 35, March 1988
ISSN 0379.0991

1992: Une Nouvelle Economie Européenne. Une évaluation des effets économiques potentiels de l'achèvement du Marché intérieur de la Communauté Européenne.

ECONOMIE EUROPEENNE, no. 35, mars 1988
ISSN 0379.0991

Europas Zukunft:
Binnenmarkt 1992

EUROPÄISCHE WIRTSCHAFT, no. 35 (in preparation)
ISBN 0379.0991

1992: Una Nuova Economia Europa

ECONOMIA EUROPEA, no. 35 (in preparation)
ISBN 0379.0991

**Research on the 'cost of non-Europe' – Basic findings of the
research**

Volume One   Basic studies: Executive summaries
Table of contents:

Series DOCUMENTS
CB–52–88–485–EN–C   ISBN 92–825–7946–8

Volume Two   Studies on the economics of integration
Table of contents:

Partial equilibrium calculations of the impact of internal market
barriers in the European Community
Conséquences macroéconomiques de l'achèvement du marché intérieur – l'enseignement des modèles macroéconomiques

Series DOCUMENTS
CB–52–88–493–EN–C   ISBN 92–825–7947–6

*Volume Three   The completion of the internal market: a survey of
European industry's perception of the likely effects*

Series DOCUMENTS
CB–52–88–502–EN–C   ISBN 92–825–7948–4

(other language versions will also be published)

The complete series of the full reports, whose Executive Summaries
are published in Volume One, will be also published by the

OFFICE FOR OFFICIAL PUBLICATIONS OF THE EURO-
PEAN COMMUNITIES
L–2985 Luxembourg

in its series 'DOCUMENTS'.